BRAINDROPS

Benn Perry

ISBN 978-1466463448

To order this book, contact your local bookseller or online at:

www.CreateSpace.com/3711242

Proudly made in the USA – Charleston, South Carolina

Cover Design – Andrea Perrine Brower
APB Illustration & Graphic Communication

Dear Michael & Susan —

I hope a few of these
BRAINDROPS tickle your fancy!

Love,
Ben

To My Soul Mate

Without you in my life I'd merely exist!

As with everything else I think, dream and do, this book is dedicated to you, Judy.

m4m

A Note to My Readers

I understand poetry is supposed to be subjective, but in my opinion, subjectivity is only tolerable to a limited degree. Poetry needs to be candy for the brain, not battery acid.

With that in mind, I decided to add a new wrinkle to my collection of personal writings, opting to follow several poems with essays that delve deeper into the thoughts that came to mind as I was putting pen to paper.

You might find yourself re-interpreting as you go, because the question "what was the author actually thinking?" is removed from the equation.

Don't get me wrong, there's nothing contained in this ana that requires the mind of a Rhodes Scholar or Mensa Member.

These pages are an amalgamation of tons of topics that have, as mentioned on the back cover, *at one time or another crossed my cranial canvas.* Foremost, they contain poems that are mixed among random thoughts, word play, full-blown soap box oratory, controlled rants and a wide range of musings. You could say it is a veritable cornucopia for your reading pleasure!

I truly hope you enjoy the time you're about to invest in reading my words. Should a few *BRAINDROPS* happen to fall on your head, and make their way happily inside…that would be pretty sweet.

Enjoy!

The stuff you're about to read…

NICKELS & DIMES----------1

WORLD SERIOUS----------5

SUCH COMPLEX LANGUAGE----------8

HOW QUICKLY ETHICS SEEM TO DIE----------9

…AND JUSTICE FOR SOME----------13

ON A LIGHTER NOTE----------18

EXCUSES, EXCUSES----------25

FAREWELL TO PARADISE----------32

11/22/63----------34

THE LITTLE GREEN MAN----------36

JUST THINK WHAT WE'D BE MISSING----------39

SINGLES BARS & COOKIE JARS----------41

FOR ALL YOU HAVE----------42

INEQUITABLE IRONIES----------43

FEAR & WAR----------46

THE U.S. GLOBAL EMPIRE----------56

DOCTOR OF DUNK----------60

More stuff you're about to read...

RHYTHM, RHYME & SONG----------61

BUT PATIENCE, DEAR DOCTOR----------62

THE KING IS IN HIS PENTHOUSE----------64

WITHOUT WARNING----------65

TELL ME TALES----------66

SOFT-BOILED CANDIDATE----------67

PHYSICAL FIT----------68

UNTIL WE BECOME THE NEWS----------69

NUCLEAR WASTE----------70

DEAR DAD----------71

THE MIRACLE NAMED DARREN----------72

DIVINE PERCEPTIONS----------81

BROKEN BARRIERS----------82

WHY BUY AT ALL?----------83

DAYTIME TRAUMA----------84

RIOT-TORN & WONDERING----------85

GOOSE BUMPS----------86

MOVIE MADNESS----------87

The last stuff you're about to read...

URGENT BULLETIN----------89

THE THINGS I LIKE----------92

WITH BLINDERS ON----------95

FREE ADVICE----------96

YOU CAN QUOTE ME ON THAT ----------98

HAPPIER NEW YEAR----------145

HOW TO FIX AMERICA----------146

CANCER----------151

BUT FIRST, THESE BRIEF DISCLAIMERS----------157

CRAZY PEOPLE----------159

PLEASE DON'T TALK ABOUT ME WHEN I'M GONE----------165

THANK YOU----------166

NICKELS & DIMES

For old desperados there are no bravados
and their week is a dreaded citation -

Since they seldom find work and most duties they'll shirk
there rarely is time for elation.

Ah, but the cats come out on Friday night
and to this end he carries his plight -

To reach for the hand that will reach back to him and
take him away to his freedom.

But the hand's never there as they continue to stare
at his worn out lapels in confusion -

And he realizes then as do most desperate men
that his life has been one grand illusion.

A nickel or dime he controls through his mime
as his body contorts for your pleasure -

For a nickel or dime will help buy him time
and time IS the ultimate treasure.

He survives just for weekends as his dream somewhat bleakens
but hangs on nonetheless out of pride -

For he knows deep inside that he truly could glide
through life as a modest folk hero.

Yet he can't help but think that what drove him to drink
was the destiny God deemed to fit him.

So the coins roll around to a beautiful sound
as they lie down to rest in his cup -

And the man feels protected as he turns to look up
to the heavens to enter his plea:

"It warms my heart to know that the world still cares so
for its desperados its culprits and sinners -

As much as it does for the rich and successful
those people we all know as WINNERS!"

_ _ _ _ _

I vividly recollect where I experienced the scene that led to writing this, my first poem. It has left an undeniable and indelible impression on me.

It was a typically scorching and inhumanly humid August afternoon in Fort Lauderdale, Florida in 1977. I was stopped at a traffic light heading northbound on Pine Island Road at State Road 84 when out of the corner of my left eye, I noticed a man, probably no older than 35 - but looking disheveled and closer to 60, standing beside a shopping cart filled with what looked for the world to me like a pile of garbage.

Mesmerized, I hadn't noticed that the light had changed, signaling me to proceed toward my destination. There were no other cars behind me, which was odd because it was the middle of the afternoon.

Maybe I was supposed to spend more time observing this phenomenon.

I'd seen panhandlers on many occasions and at dozens of different locations, but this man really held my interest.

Upon closer inspection it dawned on me that inside that Publix shopping cart was all his worldly belongings. It was one of those "there but for the grace of God goes I" moments.

When you see someone down on their luck, missing a limb, walking with a red-tipped cane or bearing some other scars that upon first presumption might serve to darken their existence by life's personal tragedies...that kind of moment.

It made me wonder about the man behind the immediate image. Had he *recently* become homeless? Had he any shelter other than that which the viaduct provided? Did he have any relatives who could help him? Did he have any friends living under similar circumstances or otherwise?

I pictured him as a former high-power executive with a major corporation that decided to cut payroll from the top down. I wondered if he was or had ever been married, if he was a parent, if he had any skills that he hadn't yet honed.

It's funny how we snap to judgment about total strangers, before coming to the realization that we have no right to do so. How can we, when we know absolutely nothing about them?

I wanted to talk to him.

I wanted to learn more about him.

Instead, I drove the few miles I had left on my journey to my apartment and wrote Nickels & Dimes; my first official poem.

In no small way, I regret having not engaged him in conversation.

Is he still dwelling under that overpass nearly 35 years later?

Did he land a job that would allow him to rest his head on a pillow at night instead of the cold, hard pavement?

Was his situation only temporary?

Was he better off on that day than he was the day before?

Maybe he didn't have those few rags to wear yesterday and things were looking brighter with each new sunrise; although I doubted as much.

Perhaps he's long since died.

Of course, and sadly, I'll never know.

WORLD SERIOUS

Remember well the World Series
when countries are ablaze -

That double-play that saved the day
and how we stood amazed.

The game is more important now
than life itself it seems -

They arbitrate for salaries
that far-exceed *our* dreams.

The dollar bill is now a part
of every inning played -

Their so-called "earned" diplomas
so worthlessly displayed.

The values and the virtues
we bestow upon our sports -

Are so damned influential
that our thinking oft' distorts.

We've put so much emphasis
on going out and winning -

That it doesn't matter who gets hurt
or if we might be sinning.

But we the fans support all this
and carry on throughout -

Even when we stop to think...
how important is an out?

One thought should soon be growing clear to us;
it's time we took our world more serious.

I wrote *World Serious* between the 1st and 15th of May in 1986. I only remember that because it was part of a *Sports Commentary* column I wrote that appeared bi-weekly in *The South Florida Review* during my "angst for athletes" phase, which, not coincidentally, began about a week after I realized ***my*** career as a centerfielder was over.

It really grated on me that a professional baseball player, or any athlete for that matter, could pull in a larger yearly income than the President of the United States of America, for Pete Rose sake. And that was 25 YEARS AGO! Since then, contracts are inked that put a mere few million bucks to shame.

Take Alex Rodriguez (and many Yankees fans are saying just that) for a fine example. Still playing baseball as of 2011 for the New York Yankees, his 10-year, $275,000,000.00 contract breaks down to some difficult to digest figures for the average Joe. Make that for ANY Joe!

Check this out:

If A-Rod plays every game of a 162 game season, at $27M per season, he earns (the "earns" part is wildly debated these days):

- **$166,666.66** *per game* (a devil of a number)
- **$18,518.51** *per inning* (not counting extra innings)
- **$52,941.17** *per at bat* @ 510 plate appearances for the season. He hasn't had an injury-free season or made that many plate appearances in a single season, yet his salary is still paid. I'd be upset if I was a New York baseball fan too!

Now, the league ***minimum***, the amount paid to ***journeymen*** ballplayers in MLB, exceeds that of the "leader of the free world" and could probably buy a few third-world countries just for kicks.

Where I might have been driven by youthful angst or even, admittedly, jealousy back then, I suppose I've numbed to it over the last couple of decades. It is the way of the jock world.

Famously, when Babe Ruth was asked by a reporter if he thought it was fair that he earned more money playing baseball in 1923 than the President, he simply replied: "Sure! I had a better year than he did!" There you have it in a nutshell.

My feelings about star athletes and their income potential remain consistent to this day.

Conversely, I think every single teacher from elementary through the college system, every blue-collar worker, every receptionist, every housewife and everyone else who makes this country tick - ought to earn more than our idolized ballplayers.

*"But we the fans support all this
and carry on throughout -*

*Even when we stop to think...
how important is an out?"*

SUCH COMPLEX LANGUAGE

Why do we call them BIGOTS
if their thinking is so small?

Why is it called a **PARA**CHUTE
when one can break our fall?

Why do we call them RACISTS
if they cross no finish lines?

Why must we call them PROPHETS
if they claim no rich designs?

Why do we call it GROWING OLD
when it looks as if we're shrinking?

Who do we call it APTITUDE
instead of simply...thinking?

Why do we call them BOXERS
when their craft is in a ring?

Why do we call them HUMMINGBIRDS
if we cannot hear them sing?

Why do we call them MISSILES
when they're built to hit their mark?

What is it God is EVENING
by turning daytime dark?

HOW QUICKLY ETHICS SEEM TO DIE

Now I know we swore we'd never air such trash on your TV
but our sponsors paid $2 MILL per spot, so please watch carefully.

With one year left in college he swore he'd not turn Pro
but their contract offered him so much...he packed his bags to go.

The company had great plans for him and hoped that he'd be loyal
but patents rarely come about...their plan's about to spoil.

My lawyer said we had a case of blatant anti-trust
but since his hefty payoff came, my case rests, collecting only dust.

Of course my dear, I promised clear "Till death do we both part"
but an uptown plastic surgeon just sowed my greedy heart.

I guarantee more MPGs and the car will soon be yours
but the formula stays etched behind some OPEC minister's doors.

So what if all of my accounts earn interest in Swiss banks
I have Exxon, Gulf and Mobil to offer heartfelt thanks.

They say that each man has his price somewhere along the way
how quickly ethics seem to die...once we're offered pay!

– – – – –

When I was a kid a *Hanna-Barbera* cartoon on TV called *The Jetsons* was my absolute favorite show. Kids can still find it on The Cartoon Network, no doubt, and, get this; much of it remains science fiction...*even to them!*

Time was supposed to change that.

Anyway, it was about a "typical" space age family with a Mom and Dad, their two kids and the family pet dog that "walked them" on a treadmill. At their immediate disposal were the most futuristic gadgets...it made every kid excited about growing up in the next quarter century.

How cool would it be to fly around from place to place, we wondered? The morning commute to and from work (we'd all probably have jobs by then, unfortunately) would be a joy instead of a Stop n' Go grind every day.

Fast forward a generation or two. Lo and behold, cars from the 1960's look more modern than today's. The "concept" vehicles paraded at auto shows throughout the world look more retro than actual cars we drove as teenagers. What's up with that?

I've long since given up the notion that I'd ever have a maid named Rosie that would have my clothes and briefcase waiting for me on the other side of the conveyor belt that took me through the washing up and shaving phase of getting ready for work (though my wife may refute that statement) but doggone it...why aren't we driving sleek, awesome looking cars?

Technology is so advanced and is advancing faster than the speed of human thought - yet there are simple creature comforts that we are unable to enjoy as a result of corporate greed and the conspicuous absence of ethics.

Unless we're living with our heads in the sand, we know without question that long ago "they" developed cars that could provide fuel economy in excess of 100 miles per gallon.

A minor amount of research will reveal proof that they existed decades ago, but, as the saying goes "every man has his price!" Or, every man **better** have his price…if he wants to remain on the green side of the grass.

No conspiracy theorist is yours truly, but if oil is the world's most essential, if not most precious commodity, what little inventor will be tolerated standing in the way of BIG OIL profiteers?

If you're expecting someone to burst on the scene saying "Hey, world…look at me, I made a car engine that runs on tap water" don't hold your breath. That person will be silenced faster than you can say "Where can I get one of those?"

So, most people that come up with brilliant, positively life-changing inventions are thwarted from sharing their products with the general public.

They either "go away" with their payoff and are never heard from again, like a smart person who wishes to live would do; or they don't "go away" with their payoff, they just GO AWAY and are never heard from again.

Which of the two would *you* choose, given that scenario?

That is of course a rhetorical question. You'd like to believe that you wouldn't be bought, that you couldn't be bought, and I suppose that is admirable.

But in the modern world you aren't being realistic…unless you have that remarkable gene flowing through your very soul that will allow you to die for what you believe in.

I wish I could say that's me, but I cannot with true conviction at this stage in my game of life. When I was in my late 20's and early 30's, all bright-eyed and ready to rock the known universe with my energy and zest for making the world a better place, maybe. Not now, to be perfectly and totally candid.

...AND JUSTICE FOR SOME

Browse on through the Internet and see if you can find
a counselor bent on fortunes won
to help you ease your mind.

It matters not the case involved or who you long to sue,
what really matters most right now
is what you have to do...

**...to assure financial freedom
once *your* case is finally through!**

Even if it means as much as suing their own mothers
the esquire goes right for the throat
each time he gets his druthers.

Of course there are exceptions to every single rule
but eight or nine times out of ten
they'll play us for the fool.

Give me green, not black and blue,
I do not feel your pain;
Accept small payments down the road...
do I appear insane?

So cash in all your stocks and bonds
your savings just as well
we'll take the money up front please
and you can go to Hell.

– – – – –

What happened to the law?

Why has it become so specialized?

Why aren't practitioners in that field held to a higher standard when it comes to defending or prosecuting their fellow human being?

I'd be willing to wager that without exception, students attend law school because they want to make a difference in the world, a positive difference.

No doubt they feel that if they can pass their Bar Exam they can eventually parlay their diploma into a career in which they would take great pride, eventually becoming respected pillars of their community.

But somewhere along the way it isn't working. Not in America at least.

Frivolous litigation clogs dockets nationwide. People are suing others over such minutia that it's unfathomable when certain cases actually make their way in front of judges and then juries.

One remedy would be to have the attorney accountable in more ways than just ethically with regard to the outcome; say financially.

But that will never happen, because lawyers, while still having the right to refuse a case, are needed on both sides of the legal fence. Public Defenders (PDs) are needed for those who cannot afford their own legal representation and Prosecutors are needed to, well...prosecute "real" perpetrators.

Getting back to the PDs, though: Given the exact set of circumstances, if not 100% of the time it has to be pretty close, the Defendant with the PD will lose...even on apparent open and shut cases where his or her client should win. Why? Because that defendant cannot afford to pay an attorney that will put in the due diligence required to prove their innocence.

However, if the Defendant happens to be someone in the spotlight, either a public figure in the wide world of sports, entertainment or other arena - that Defendant's chances of acquittal are probably close to the same 100% percent as the man on the street's chances of being sent up the river.

Try walking tipsily out of your local watering hole one evening and getting behind the wheel of your 1992 Hoopdee and see how far you get.

Try walking tipsily out of your local watering hole one evening in your brand new Mercedes Benz CL 600 and getting behind the wheel and see how far you get, legally speaking.

There is a clear double standard at play.

In more times than you can imagine mirror situations played out; the only difference being the stature of the person involved in the crime of driving while under the influence of alcohol or drug du jour.

The result going in favor of the intoxicated party having a "Do you know who I am?" name is disturbingly predictable.

Money plays a gigantic role in this part of our society too.

Clearly, in **both cases** the driver needs to go straight to jail without passing go and without collecting $200 – on the FIRST OFFENSE! Sound harsh? Some countries execute in such cases!

I know people that haven't learned a lesson even after being given the opportunity to stay out of prison. Second and third offenses finally led to incarceration. And, one second offense involved the killing of three innocent people.

Anyone who puts others' lives in jeopardy by taking to the road while under the influence needs to be put in a place where they cannot harm anyone else; particularly an innocent and sober fellow driver.

As for frivolous lawsuits, we could do well by taking the lead of Great Britain. In England, frivolous lawsuits are becoming rarer; because if the Counsellor or Barrister takes on a case and his or her client loses, *the client pays all the court costs.*

That way, we can still have our system of jurisprudence, however, with severe ramifications hanging in the balance it might make those who are out to make a fast buck think twice or thrice before hopping aboard the Litigious Express!

The worst part about our legal system is that you are not going to court to have justice served; you are going in the hope that you have the best lawyer. If you do, you win. If you don't, you lose. It can't get any simpler than that.

If you believe in equality under the law you still believe in the tooth fairy and that O. J. Simpson spent every minute from the time his murder trial was over until he went to jail after being convicted under a civil suit - searching for the killer of his wife, Nicole and her waiter friend, Ron Goldman.

Caps on damages for medical malpractice cases might have made a dent in frivolous lawsuits, but didn't do much to lower fees charged by the medical profession; nor did caps lower insurance premiums for the patient or costs for malpractice insurance for doctors and surgeons.

We tend to only see the most glaringly frivolous lawsuits; the ones where idiots spill hot coffee on their laps and go after McDonalds…and win millions.

It is those types of "awards" that have people stopping short at traffic lights in order to have unsuspecting drivers slam into them from behind – so they can collect their small fortune from their whiplashes.

And we wonder why auto insurance is barely affordable for the average citizen!

Instead of going on a chapter-long rant about insurance companies, I think I'll save that subject for my next book, an exposé which I'll title *They Bet You Won't Die.*

Disclaimer:

I have friends and family that are practicing attorneys. They are the exceptions to the rule noted both in the poem and in the diatribe that followed it.

Gregg, Gary, Dayna, Billie, Harry, Marlene and Cliff…you guys have not only taken and passed The Bar, you've elevated it. I am thankful that you are making a positive difference through your work and hopeful that aspiring lawyers take their cue from the likes of you. That isn't to say that your industry still isn't a hot mess, though! ☺

ON A LIGHTER NOTE

Enough about lawyers and insurance and matters depressing, it's time for a little pun and entertainment.

Far from a *words*mith, I still like *them* and have fun coining my own. Many of these seem obvious to me. I'm predicting they'll be appearing in lexicons the world over by 2129.

We should all live to see that day.

Amen, and let's get started, shall we?

– – – – –

If someone makes a stupid comparison that really bugs you, are they making an **annoylogy**?

Or: Wouldn't you call a container that stores all of your most puzzling questions a **quandary basket**?

Or: If you appreciate the fact that someone shared their reasons for being extremely upset with you, would you say **thangst**?

Or: Is a guy that prefers to be nerdy all by himself an **independork**?

Or: Does buying a new car make a person more **motorvated** to make payments?

Or: Would you say that a product that is solid and dependable is **reliabuilt**?

Or: If they named a new hemorrhoid cream **Correctum**, would YOU buy it?

Or: Do overzealous ministers have **Methodists** to their madness?

Or: You know when your buddy shakes your hand with that thing that gives you a shock, would that be considered an **electrick**?

Or: Would being able to watch 3 or more major teams playing on TV in the same day provide a **sportgasm** to the lucky fan in question?

Or: Shouldn't a heart valve that has trouble flowing be called a **ventrickle**?

Or: If fertilizer is meant to grow grass, what would you call something you sprinkle on your lawn to promote weed growth...**tantilizer**? Actually, that would be a good name for a sunning lotion.

Or: Is someone quick to point out our flaws **complimeanery**?

Or: Would a busybody from the Far East be called an **Orienta**?

Or: Shouldn't they call surgery to remove the funny bone a **hystericalectomy**?

Or: Is someone who helps you finish your meal an **associ-ate**?

Or: If everyone stayed away from the polls on Voting Day would that be an **elecshun**?

Or: Let's call those gaudy, bejeweled things that hang off some women's ear lobes **chandelierings**!

Or: Would a pilot that has to have something in his mouth all the time be called a **paciflyer**?

Or: Say you had an idea that you tossed aside, would you call it your **outvention**?

Or: Someone with a sense of humor that runs for office should be considered **politickle**?

Or: Shouldn't a person with an overly dry sense of humor be called **aridiculous**?

Or: Shouldn't chefs be required to get a **culinoscopy** every few years after they reach 50?

Or: Shouldn't something that is 180 degrees different from something else be called its **etisoppo**? You have 30 seconds to try to figure that one out.

Or: Would someone who has performed the same role on stage many times be a **reactor**?

Or: Shouldn't our Birthday really be called our Anniversary? We only have ONE Birthday, don't we?

Or: If 15% is a decent gratuity, would a **grathreeity** be a really, really nice tip?

Or: Is someone that ponders your vision **philosoptical**?

Or: Would a rodent writer that wishes to keep his identity concealed be considered **anonymouse**?

Or: Is someone that says they've worn glasses for as long as they can remember being **retrospectacle**?

Or: Is a go-getter type person that establishes a cow chip company being **entremanureal**?

Or: I think a great name for biographies about athletes would be **jockumentaries**?

Or: Would a Norwegian that is drunk in public be considered **Scandinebriated**?

Or: Why aren't they called **getters** and the people to whom they bring food be the ones called **waiters**?

Or: Bank robbers that take every penny out of the bank should be called **absolooters**.

Or: Someone that gives you something expecting something in return should be called **charitabull**.

Or: Would a game that's just a little more exciting than tennis be called **elevenis**?

Or: For that matter, would we call a singer that's a tad more prolific than The King...**Twelvis**?

Or: If something that is awe-inspiring is wonderful, shouldn't something twice as awe-inspiring be **twoderful**?

Or: Why is it called manure and not **womanure**? Why isn't the city called **Womanhattan**? **Womanipulating** or **womandate** instead? And, shouldn't it be **Womanischevitz Whine**, not Manischevitz Wine?

Or: Why do we call it **GROWING OLD** when it looks as if we're shrinking? You'd get that if you read page 8 by now; and you should have, considering it was 13 pages ago and you couldn't possibly have been bored that early on in this book – hopefully!

Or: If one is completely overzealous about religion would they be a **fundamentalcase**?

Or: If someone gets back at you for getting back at them for getting back at you would that be **rereretaliation**?

Or: By the same token, if you say the same thing over and over and over again wouldn't that be **rerereiteration**?

Or: I know, let's call a cool elderly water buffalo a **hipoldpatamus**.

Or: If you found yourself eating out at the same restaurant quite often wouldn't you eventually get a feeling of **dè-jâ-food**?

Or: Why is it called **outsourcing** instead of "giving away jobs to other countries because we are incredibly greedy and don't care about our own citizens enough to keep them employed?" I know that wasn't word play, but it was a social commentary that was on my mind, so I stuck in here.

Or: If your intellectual acuity was of the lowest extreme would you be **monumentally retarded**?

Or: Why don't they just call the act of getting something back **covery**? Wouldn't getting it back a SECOND time be **recovery**? Like upholster and reupholster, right? Actually it should be called **downholster**, shouldn't it? No, that would be a protective case for a gun made out of goose feathers. Never mind.

Or: If a handle is named because you grasp it with your hand, shouldn't a pedal be called a **footle**? And a petal should be a small stroke you rub on the back of a puppy or a kitten in your lap, not a part of a flower. Besides, a *flower* is a sink or a river or a stream or a nose with a bad head cold.

Or: If tendering money for your bills is called payments, why not call the cash you lay out for candy **paymints** or for certain pies, **paymince**?

Or: I would call someone who gives away great sums of money on South Beach **philantropical**, wouldn't you? However, if that same person was upset with all the troubles money brought them and used that as their motivation for giving away their money, could it be said that he or she only did it because they were **philanthropissed**?

Or: Is using your leisure time to squirt water out of your mouth called taking a **respit**?

Or: Why isn't **oar** just spelled **or**, like all along the left hand column, but without the colon or comma? Speaking of that, if a **comma** is meant to represent a short pause in a sentence and a **coma** is a very long pause, shouldn't **comma** be spelled **coma** and vice-versa?

Or: Would someone who cannot stomach other peoples' lowest extremities be **lacktoes** intolerant or would they simply lack toes tolerance?

Or: **Mistressmind**?

Or: Would a homeless dude who isn't giving you too much detail about something he's rambling about be on a **vaguerant**?

Or: If we went hunting and brought home more than the legal limit, would that be considered an act of **malpheasants**?

Or: Doctors have **patients** until it comes time for you to pay their bill, then they lose their **patience**?

Or: If something very coincidental happened to someone else, wouldn't it be called **theyronic**? Then again, if something very coincidental happened to one's self, shouldn't it be called **meronic**, not **ironic**? I'm just trying to be grammatically correct. Then again...shouldn't it be **grammartically** correct?

Maybe it's all a little **Mo**ronic - or is that Larry or Curlyronic? PLEASE, make it STOP!

Or: Would a numbers wizard that decided he wasn't going to add, subtract, multiply or divide anymore be called a **mathmatishun**?

Or: If you are a holy thinker and behave in a holy manner in the first place why not simply say you're **ligious**? And instead of "born again" - under those circumstances you can call yourself **religious**?

Or: Are those guys in the NBA with shaved heads **basketbald**?

Or: We should call smart Catholics **Intelligentiles**.

Or: What do you think they'll call the last country standing; **ExtermiNATION**?

Or: I think they should call the ovation guys give to dancers in topless joints **menapplause**!

Have you ever realized that if you spell the words **THE** and **IRS** together you get **THEIRS**?

No wonder they're the ones that get all the money come tax time! It was meant to be **THEIRS** all along!

EXCUSES, EXCUSES

I could have been a DIPLOMAT
but had no time to talk.

I could have been an ASTRONAUT
but motion made me balk.

I could have been a LION TAMER
but allergies prevailed.

I could have been an AUTHOR
but my keyboard always failed.

I could have been a FIGHTER
but my trunks would not stay up.

I could have run with the BIG DOGS
but I was a tiny pup.

I could have been a HOCKEY STAR
but I couldn't stand on skates.

I could have been a BAREBACK RIDER
but I'd have to sit on crates.

I could have been a DANCER
but both my feet turned left.

I could have been a SUMO WRESTLER
but lacked essential heft.

I could have been an ACTOR
but failed to take directions.

I could have been the PRESIDENT
but lost all my elections.

I could have been a RICH MAN
if money grew on trees.

I could have been a LAWYER
but I wouldn't charge the fees.

I could have been a SOLDIER
if I knew what war was for.

I could have been a SURGEON
but I couldn't stand the gore.

I could have been a CAPTAIN
had my ship stayed in the tub.

I could have been an EAGLE SCOUT
but I couldn't get past Cub.

I could have been a SINGER
if every song was short.

I could have been a PAINTER
if my easel gave support.

I could have been a TEACHER
but kids just drove me mad.

I could have been a JUNIOR
had they named me after Dad.

I could have been a SCHOLAR
but I couldn't get through books.

I could have been a FISHERMAN
were I not afraid of hooks.

I could have been INVENTING
had I worked into the night.

I could have been a PREACHER
but I saw no guiding light.

I could have been a QUARTERBACK
but armchair was my style.

I could have been a CIRCUS CLOWN
but rarely cracked a smile.

I could have been a WRITER
but my pen ran out of ink.

I could have been more THOUGHTFUL
if I didn't have to think.

I could have been an OPTIMIST
if my outlook was reversed.

I could have been a GENIUS
but I guess my brain was cursed.

I could have been an ANALYST
but my couch kept breaking down.

I could have been the MAYOR
but was scared to work downtown.

I could have been an ORDERLY
but my thoughts got too confused.

I could have been a UNION HEAD
had I paid my yearly dues.

I could have been a POET
but the words all came out wrong.

I could have been a CHAMPION
but competitions last too long.

I could have been a GOURMET CHEF
but onions made me weep.

I could have been a DREAMER
but I couldn't fall asleep.

I could have been the ENVY of all my childhood peers
but excuses always led the way throughout my childhood years!

— — — — —

This is my favorite poem, bar none. It is meant to be inspirational and hard-hitting at the same time. It is intended to move my readers to action; not embarrass or chastise them for their past inability to achieve a goal.

It came from the deepest part of my heart that demands of me to do whatever I can while I'm on this planet to help others; regardless of personal times that may seem difficult.

My hope is that the words in this poem will turn people inward, providing a personal sense of discovery and reawakening, which will allow them to embark on even grander dreams TODAY, regardless of their age or presumed limitations.

At some point in each of our lives we manufacture "reasons" (which are actually excuses) for failing to achieve a goal or direct our own destiny.

One of the greatest spiritual benefits afforded me through working as a certified Empowermind trainer and workshop presenter (Empowermind.com) - is having the chance to make an impact on students of all ages that are struggling in school or in life in general – by reciting *Excuses, Excuses* for them at the end of the second and final session of those workshops - and leaving them with a strong "I can do anything I put my mind to" sense of confidence.

But excuses manage to rule most of our days, don't they?

When we become adults we find ourselves in jobs we can't stand, in relationships we abhor, and in situations we wish were different. And because they are what they are instead of what we'd hoped they would be - we come up with excuse after excuse to justify our very existence.

Perhaps this poem will rekindle that creative spark that your life needs to get you back on track, to move you to take control of the things that matter most in your life, and, through hard work - help you begin to realize some of your dreams.

You can turn the page in your life's journey as simply as you can turn the pages in this book. The *seed* of your dream is already planted; all you have to do is *cultivate* a plan to ultimately make it your reality.

CAUTION!

"Never share your dreams with anyone unless you know without question they will be a positive part of your journey toward achieving them." ~ Me

What might it do to your confidence if you share your dreams with someone you've always looked up to for words of wisdom and they tell you to forget about it, that no matter what, it won't work? Clearly it can shatter your dreams, if you allow it.

Loved ones can be the worst people to share your dreams with as they tend to (in what they feel is their most loving means of showing true concern and support) throw a wet blanket over them; insisting that it's because they don't want you to experience the pain associated with **failure**, that perhaps they might have felt.

Heed these next words, no matter how old you are or how experienced you might be with the lack of achieving positive results:

There are no failures, only stepping stones to success!

Steven Jobs, the Co-Founder, Chairman and CEO of Apple, Inc. passed away after a protracted battle with cancer on October 5, 2011. Eulogies appeared on every TV station and on countless Internet blogs, airing his speeches and general messages to the public.

I found the following quote attributed to him that I'd like to share with you:

Its header read…*What's your excuse?*

"Your time is limited, so don't waste it living someone else's life. Don't be trapped by dogma – which is living with the results of other people's thinking. Don't let the noise of others' opinions drown out your own inner voice. And most important, have the courage to follow your heart and intuition. They somehow already know what you truly want to become. Everything else is secondary."

~ Steven Jobs

Whenever the time comes that you realize **your dreams** – know that they only became possible the day you stopped making excuses!

FAREWELL TO PARADISE

Well now they've gone and done it, build a K-Mart in the sticks;
no more scents of sandalwood, just leveled dirt and bricks.

No more squirrels or rabbits, they've chased them all away;
a naturalist's disaster, not "progress" as "they" say.

A shopping center overdose is taking root today;
no more vacant lots or parks where kids can play.

Crackling bonfires lit the night; ghost stories filled the air;
it's tough to picture parking lots and storefronts over there.

But the hardhats and the dozers and the cement trucks prevailed;
our planners and commissioners are the ones that truly failed.

The plants are gone, no signs of life, just K-Marts everywhere;
and to those who try to justify it...

I still don't think it's fair!

– – – – –

Some of the greatest pearls of wisdom imparted to me by my Mom were: "Stop to look around at nature; it's so beautiful, and one day there won't be much of it left!"

I used to tease her when she'd point out the changing leaves of autumn, saying stuff like "Oh, Mom...LOOK, isn't that blade of grass or brown leaf with the holes in it simply glorious?"

She'd laugh; knowing I was only partly teasing her; still without uttering a word I could hear her thinking "He'll get it one day!"

As usual, she was right. I *think* I started appreciating nature while she was still alive, but since she's passed I've been much more conscious of my changing environment and am reminded of those so-sensitive-to-Mother Earth words that rolled eloquently off her tongue back in the day.

Nature seems to be a lot further away for most of us now. What was once outside our front door is a half hour drive away. Seasons are hard to mark when you live in the southernmost states and you find that *before you know it the years fly by*.

I recollect a Chamber of Commerce evening spent on a charter boat ride along the Intracoastal Waterway that found me chatting with the captain, a young man in is mid 20's, I guessed.

We were discussing how time flies and he told me a story that confirmed it perfectly. He received a phone call from his mother the other day asking him when he was heading back up to Ohio for a visit.

He sighed and somewhat exasperatingly said "Gee, Ma, I was just there last July, for the 4th, remember?"

"No, son…next month it will be *three and a half years since you've been back!*" she reminded him.

So, yeah…walk outside and smell the air if it's still clean where you are, and, for my Mom's sake…check out the falling leaves of gold, red and yellow the next time you get the chance.

PS: I have nothing against K-Mart. I needed a recognizable metaphor. Besides, it's still my Dad's favorite place to shop!

11/22/63

I came home from school for lunch
and found my family in front of the TV.

Everyone looked as if their tear ducts
had taken a terrible beating.

I turned to the tube that delivered the news:

"I repeat" the man said, "President Kennedy is dead!"

It was the first time I'd ever seen
the whole world cry together like that.

At nine, it's hard to bare witness to such a sight.

The worst thing was the replays,
those slow-motion clips.

The rest of that winter was gray.

I found myself wondering, even at that young age,
how anyone could be allowed to live on this wonderful planet
with hate in their heart or murder on their mind.

The "Six O'clock Report" took on a different
meaning for me from that moment on.

No longer was it just a game of cops and robbers
or a bang-bang, shoot-em-up fantasy show!

$- - - - -$

Unfortunately tragedies have their way of serving to let us mark time more frequently than happier events.

We remember where we were when our team won the World Championship - for sure.

We rejoice at the memory of high school or college graduation - certainly.

With pride we look back on our first automobile - indeed.

But the haunting natural disasters that occur like tsunamis, earthquakes, tornadoes and floods have us looking back in bewilderment, while something as heinous as the murder of the most familiar public figure in the entire country has us looking back in anger and disbelief; leaving us outraged.

The effect that such an event as the President of the United States of America being assassinated on TV has on a boy of nine cannot be measured. It stays with him forever.

Everyone that was alive remembers exactly where they were when the Twin Towers of the World Trade Center came down on what is referred to simply as 9/11. Not just because it forever changed our way of thinking about the safety and security of our own shores but because of the vivid pictures that were instantly available across every media outlet imaginable.

Like coming home to a house full of crying parents and neighbors, that sort of cataclysmic disaster is engrained in our souls and psyches for the duration of our earthly days as well.

THE LITTLE GREEN MAN

It was just an ordinary Sunday
until the knock came at my door.

I asked if he was frightened
and he calmly asked "What for?"

This little green man about three-feet-two
was stretching out his legs;

"The trip took 15 light years" he said
"and they've stiffened into pegs!"

When I asked him why he chose my house
he pointed toward the street;

"I had to land it somewhere
and those pine trees looked pretty neat."

The questions started flowing
about the Earth and then of Mars;

The little man sounded sacred
as he talked about the stars.

He told us that he longed to travel
when he was just a child;

That those 15 light years weren't so bad
and his trip was rather mild.

Too many of his friends grew up
and never took to flight;

And the fact that he had broken free
was reason to delight.

He longed for open spaces
and was starved for friendly faces;

So we asked him in for dinner
and in awe we took our places.

The most amazing thing about him
was he carried no protection;

He never feared us for a moment,
he was sure of *his* selection.

We spent an hour on dinner
and then he turned to go;

He thanked us for the fuel
and for letting our feelings flow.

And even though his visit
came abruptly to an end...

We learned to treat a stranger as if he were a friend!

– – – – –

Yes, I DO believe in life on other planets. How incredibly pompous is it to think that of the billions upon billions of stars in the multitude of galaxies and beyond - there is but a solitary planet that has forms of life inhabiting it and it just so happens to be ours?

I've never had the thrill of seeing an unidentified flying object, nor have I had the misfortune of being abducted and probed by aliens; although I do know someone who was.

The stories he tells and the finite details into which he delves would raise the neck hair on any disbeliever.

I tried to convince him to write a book about his incredible ordeal, and, perhaps one day he will. Trust me, it will have you at the very least questioning certain inexplicable phenomena.

The longer I live I marvel at the **devolution** our planet appears to be going through; and the more unequivocally convinced I've become that we Earthlings cannot possibly be the **only**, let alone **most "intelligent"** representation found amid the **"Googolplexian"** miles that we call outer space.

Do you think the notion of limitless search possibilities is where the brains at **Google** came up with the name for their company?

I do.

Then again, I also fervently believe in flying saucers and extra-terrestrials!

JUST THINK WHAT WE'D BE MISSING

If it weren't for drugs there'd never be dealers.
If it weren't for faith there'd never be healers.

If it weren't for dough we wouldn't have bakers.
If it weren't for land there wouldn't be acres.

If it weren't for words there'd never be books.
If it weren't for jewels we wouldn't have crooks.

If it weren't for ships we wouldn't build harbors.
If it weren't for trees there couldn't be arbors.

If it weren't for lies we'd never be confessed.
If it weren't for clothing how could we get dressed?

If it weren't for nations we wouldn't need leaders.
If it weren't for policemen we'd never catch speeders.

If it weren't for hearts we wouldn't have loving.
If it weren't for elevators there'd be much less shoving.

If it weren't for the hero who'd reap the reward?
If it weren't for money what could we afford?

If it weren't for taxes we'd keep all our wages.
If it weren't for genius we wouldn't have sages.

If it weren't for feelings we couldn't show pain.
If it weren't for the bridge there'd be no refrain.

If it weren't for choice we'd make no decision.
If it weren't for bifocals we'd have double vision.

If it weren't for motion pictures life would just stand still.
If it weren't for jealous relatives we wouldn't need a will.

If it weren't for tobacco they'd roll fewer smokes.
If it weren't for good humor we couldn't tell jokes.

If it weren't for strangers how could we make friends?
If it weren't for beginnings we wouldn't have ends.

SINGLES BARS & COOKIE JARS

Breakfast in suburbia, but daddy's not around,
the single mother struggles to make sure they're safe and sound;

Then rushes off the little ones so the bus won't have to wait,
and spends a few quiet moments sipping coffee until eight.

The office is a daily grind and often frays her nerves;
a two-week-long vacation is what the girl deserves.

She dials home at break time, around ten minutes after three,
"There's cookies in the cookie jar" and "Wait inside for me!"

It's hard to have composure as punch-out time draws near
she puts together dinner in her mind until it's clear.

As she greets them at the front door steps and carries them inside
she feels a sense of dignity, accomplishment and pride.

Dinner's done and bedtime comes, but gets here all too soon
she has not time to talk to them as they rush off to their room.

The babysitter rings the bell and makes her way inside
off to the singles bar she goes while swallowing that pride.

Her late return depletes her purse, but the babysitter smiles
her marathon is winding down after all those lonesome miles.

Another day, another night, the weeks and months race by
she tries to fall asleep again as a tear drops from her eye.

What went wrong and what went right and why the empty spaces
why did all the people at the bar have empty faces?

Soon the madness passes as she reaches for the sheet
only one thing's missing or her life would be complete.

FOR ALL YOU HAVE

You sit back at the table and presume you're unable
to change the life that you're leading;
and your wine washes down past a mouth etched afrown,
as though your poor heart was bleeding.

And as you lie down to sleep with your wife tucked in neat
beside you through thick and through thin;
you think to yourself of great fame and wealth,
and the company you'll someday be keeping.

But reflect just before you slam shut your door
on the man who is out in the cold;
with none of the joys that your life employs,
he's the colt who got lost from his fold.

The midnight buffet that you'll soon throw away
could feed him for more than a week;
No mattress for his head, sleeps in alleys instead,
no sight for the timid or meek.

It might do you some good and indeed really should
to give thanks for how well you've been blessed;
knowing it's prayed for each day in a desperate way,
but please…try not to become too depressed.

INEQUITABLE IRONIES

Billionaires lockout millionaires and prevent them from taking part in professional games while the homeless search for discarded newspapers in order to cushion their heads as they try to find sleep on the cold pavement of an urban ghetto in Anywhere, USA.

Mothers and fathers lose sons and daughters fighting in wars overseas to protect the freedoms we hold so dear back home, but while on leave from one of their tours of duty those "warriors" over there are still considered "children" over here and cannot order a beer with a friend down at the neighborhood bar. You must be 18 to fight and die for your country, but 21 to knock back a cold brew. I never could get my head around that one!

Republicans and Democrats argue in Congress no matter the issue and the only thing they can agree on is the 2-Party system; while Independent thinkers are cast aside as bloc-busters or outsiders who stand no chance of winning even the smallest town election.

People prefer collecting unemployment because it's better than working at a job that pays less after taxes – which ends up costing small business owners more money in unemployment taxes, keeps them understaffed and leaves no money for benefits to be paid to their remaining employees.

Water costs more per gallon by the bottle than gasoline and the Earth is made up of 70% of the stuff. Meanwhile, gasoline costs 7¢ per gallon in Venezuela and hovers around $4.00 per gallon in America; the land with an abundance of natural resources that could entirely eliminate the need for oil - foreign or domestic.

Local farmers are starving while exporting their produce to neighboring countries at a cost that returns far less than if they grew their crops solely for the consumption of the American consumer; all the while jobs are being outsourced to factories that export goods to us with far less quality control mechanisms in place.

We spend much more time watching television, glued to our PS3's, laptops, iPods and Tablets than we do having quiet dinners at home with our family or exercising a sound regimen of physical fitness; and wonder why the brains of our youth are dulling and heart attacks and obesity rates are at epidemic levels.

Anyone in the entertainment industry can blow 5 times the legal limit for alcohol, be deemed completely inebriated, cuss out the police officer pulling them over and threaten bystanders if either of them dares answer the interrogated party's question "Do you know who I am?" incorrectly. While the average slob who struggles to make ends meet would spend the night in jail awaiting their fate for a first offense of the same magnitude – because the arresting officers actually *don't* know who *we* are!

Even our double standards have double standards. We make exceptions *for* instead of examples *of* the limelight basking superstars who know full well that as long as they can still drive the ball out of the park, hit an outside jumper to beat the buzzer, throw a football through a wall from 30 yards out or make a decent action flick – they are beyond reproach and will suffer a mere slap on the wrist and a few seconds of public ridicule – ridicule from that same public that will go out the following night to see them step up to the plate, walk out on the court, grace the gridiron or attend the debut down at the local cinema complex. We, the fan, complain about the preferential treatment, then immediately turn around and ensure that it continues.

We have thousands upon thousands of people who are so hell bent on the "right to life" that they blow up clinics, killing innocent medical staff in the process.

Much like looting urban stores as if to make a statement during race rioting, that never made any sense to me...protect life so that only YOU can take it away? These are the very people who would line up to pull the switch on "Old Sparky" or watch the condemned die in their local gas chamber.

A man breaks into the shop that you worked your whole life to develop; stealing merchandise and the cash register. To make certain it never happens again you spend more of your hard-earned funds on a security system as a deterrent. But you get robbed again! Preparing for the inevitable next time, you buy a weapon to protect yourself and your investment. In the process of trying to take everything from you a third time, you shoot and severely wound the perpetrator. He sues you and wins!

To quote professional boxing promoter and convicted manslaughter "victim" Don King:

"Only in America!"

FEAR & WAR

First, FEAR!

It's really a chicken or the egg scenario with me as it relates to terrorism.

My memory is clear how we used to have air raid drills in elementary school; how we'd march down into the basement that doubled as our bomb shelter.

What did we know? It was FUN! To interrupt all of our classes, no matter what time of the day and no matter what class (unless it was Gym) was the coup of the month.

If we worked it the right way, if the regular bad kids got out of line enough times, we could milk that into nearly an hour away from our studies.

The threat of a Russian invasion was force fed to us and at that impressionable age we believed every word they told us. I cannot remember a single person ever posing the question "Do you think Russian kids think WE are the bad guys?"

So those threats left substantial fear in our hearts. If we weren't prepared, we'd end up being vaporized…although hiding under our wooden desks was the safest thing to do in the event of a nuclear holocaust, apparently.

We lived with that fear into our late teenage years, the years when many of us were drafted into the military to fight a war in a tiny place called Viet Nam that was a, putting it mildly, rather unpopular one.

In those days the military draft system was in place and that draft was run by, of all the luck, a lottery drawing. That's right, the chance that you might be sent to war was dependent entirely upon the number that popped up at the Selective Service System Draft Board.

Here's how it worked:

A day and month was recorded on blue plastic capsules; representatives of the Selective Service System drew the capsules at random from a large container. Each birth date was given a number based on the order in which they were chosen.

Luck being the four-letter word as it was for me in that instance, my Random Sequence Number or lottery number was 60. I wasn't expecting it to be 365, but SIXTY?

I was torn. Remember, this was a totally unpopular war. Protesters were lining the streets of every city in America demanding that the Viet Nam conflict come to an end. Should I enlist in the Navy, which promised to be a simpler gig than the Army or the Marines; or should Dad sneak me across the Canadian border in the trunk of his black convertible Dodge, Polara?

Summoning whatever nerve existed in this frightened 18-year olds existence; I paid a visit to the local Navy recruiter. A pitch came at me so fast and furious it would have impressed both Nolan Ryan and Justin Verlander.

The recruiter was SO GOOD at scaring me into what would happen if I didn't sign up that I could barely see straight. He said, "Well, son, all ya gotta do is sign right here and we'll get you off to basic training at Great Lakes by the end of the month!"

"Uh…not so fast, Sir" I said inside my head. But to him I said "Well, that sounds great. I'm gonna go home and think about it and I'll come back. Are you here tomorrow?" As if I didn't know!

With the kind of Drill Instructor's tone I'd only seen in the movies, he barked *"Son, there's two kinds of people in this world. There's the kind that can make up their mind and the kind that can't. Which one are YOU?"*

Thinking on my feet I said *"I'm the one who CAN make up his mind, Sir…and I AM OUTTA HERE!"*

I ran so fast out of that recruiting center that he's probably still coughing up the burned rubber my sneakers left behind.

Now what? Canada? So many times you'd hear stories about how fathers would try to smuggle their sons over the border, and when they got caught the sons would go to jail for draft evasion and the smuggling dad would have a greater sentence or penitence to pay.

FEAR made me "think" about enlisting.

FEAR made me "think" about hiding in Dad's trunk for a ride into Windsor, Ontario.

And FEAR had me worrying what would happen if I didn't go and fight for my country; because without soldiers we would be in "danger" of losing our freedoms. It worked.

FEAR, made me afraid; again!

I left out a part that needs to be filled in. When I initially was granted my draft status I was classified 1-H, which meant that only in the event of extreme emergency would I be called to active duty. Still, that "possibility" looming was unsettling. So, I decided to file for CO Status, which stood for Conscientious Objector. A CO would be the LAST person to be called upon to serve, and to me that represented my ticket out of this ridiculous armed conflict. Cool, I figured…CO is for ME!

I petitioned the draft board in the spring of 1973 to change my status and promptly, I mean REAL PROMPTLY, as in two days, I received a questionnaire that required me to substantiate WHY I was requesting a change to CO status. No kidding, it must have been a 200 page booklet.

Many of the questions challenged my faith, challenged my background, challenged my overall belief system, challenged my integrity and honesty and, ultimately, challenged my sense of attention to detail.

But I immersed myself in it for a couple of weeks, determined to be a CO. I was better than halfway through answering the questions when the shock of my life occurred. On page 122 (or whatever page it was) there was a rubber stamped note that read:

"This booklet must be filled out in its entirety and returned on or before May 1, 1973!"

HOLY COOKED CANADIAN GOOSE, BATMAN!

It was already May 10th and I wasn't close to being finished. I figured instead of taking any more time, I'd just mail it off and hope for the best.

The best did not happen. A quick two days later I received my reclassification in a terse letter that read:

Dear Mr. Perry,

Due to your failure to comply with the time constraints with regard to your reclassification questionnaire, the Board has reclassified you from 1-H to 1-A.

The next Random Sequence drawing will be held on July 15th. You will be contacted by the Draft Committee a short time thereafter for immediate reporting instructions.

And I'm pretty sure they didn't sign it...

Sincerely,

Your pals at the Selective Service System

The only part of that letter I recollect verbatim was the words **"the Board has reclassified you from 1-H to 1-A."**

For those not in the know, a 1-A classification was as close as you could come to impending doom. If *anyone* broke wind in Southeast Asia, *your* behind was going to the front lines!

Panic set in, which is a bi-product of FEAR. The rest of that summer I was worrying when exactly I'd get called up and I was actually preparing my own eulogy to be read when I lost my life fighting overseas.

By early September of that same year they had already drawn up to #48. Considering they drew numbers at a rate of 15 to 20 per month – my number was due to come up the next time they pulled...around September 14, 1973.

That is when luck reared its good, nay GREAT side, for yours truly. Almost concurrent with saying my farewells to my family and friends - the wonderful but theretofore much maligned, but now incredibly fantastic (in my opinion) President Richard Millhouse Nixon ***ENDED THE FREAKING DRAFT!***

FEAR turned to elation. I was staying home, able to pursue the career of my dreams; or collect unemployment if I felt so inclined. What bliss, and how wonderful familiar ground felt to walk on.

And now, WAR:

I have to seriously believe that if you polled a hundred million people and asked them to check either A or B in response to the following questions, 100% would select B.

Which of the following would you prefer?

   A. Being killed
   B. Living a long and peaceful life

Which would you rather see your son become?

   A. A soldier on the front line
   B. A professional athlete

If given the choice would you

   A. Hide out for 20 years in a bomb shelter
   B. Water your lawn and drink lemonade on your front porch

Do you know or know anyone who knows anyone that would honestly select A as any of their answers to the above?

Of course, you don't. SO WHY DO WE HAVE WAR?

It's a fairly simple answer, one that we all know. We fight wars because it is a financially rewarding thing to do. It is financially rewarding to the military installation alone, but it is financially rewarding - and big guys making big money is what it's all about.

Who cares if they do things differently from a societal standpoint in Russia than they do in Australia, than they do in Canada, than they do in Spain, than they do in England, than they do in Israel, than they do in Italy, than they do in Czechoslovakia, than they do in the United States, than they do in the Middle East?

Really, who cares? Like those too blind to see the possibility of life on other planets, why are we so blind as to not see that other nations wish to live their lives on their own terms?

Why it is so hard for us to fathom that socialism may work in certain parts of the world, even if it's not quite our cup of tea defies explanation.

Why can't we fathom that communism might be perfect for a people, even though we're completely opposed to the prospect of that kind of lifestyle?

Why do we "invade" other countries in an attempt to push our version of democracy down their throats? Isn't the very intention of democracy to give the people the freedom to make their own choices?

The Israelis have it right. They are defending themselves at all costs. They are NEVER the aggressor. They are NEVER the antagonist. They fire when fired upon, and, unfortunately for their

52

enemy, which is comprised of the entire rest of the Middle East, their weaponry is more precise and lethal than all of the other countries combined. I suppose if you lived as a people with the idea that there is nothing your neighbor would rather do than kill you – you'd get pretty good at defending yourself too.

Having said that, and being an ally of Israel and ANY country on the planet that wishes to be safe and secure and free from tyranny, I say it is time to pull out of that part of the world entirely and forever.

We have this propensity for entering battles that cannot be won. The percentage of wars and deaths since the dawn of humankind that can be attributed to organized religion is ridiculously high, which makes it as hypocritical as it can possibly get. Religions preach peace and prosperity and wage war against people with varying religious and political beliefs. Why? So they can make the whole world believers in their tenets and dogmata?

Atheists and agnostics have it right. They don't try to spread atheism, they just want to be left alone to believe or disbelieve whatever and however they choose.

Simply put, if you leave people alone, as long as they don't spend their time plotting your demise…what could be so wrong with letting them be? I guess that makes me an atheist or agnostic. At least I have that *kindly leave me alone* attitude.

If I abide by the laws of the land under which I live, if I am a contributing member of society, if I have something to offer that will help my neighbor live a better life…why do I have to subscribe to any particular religious group or practice their faith?

53

The trillions of dollars we spend occupying other territories around the globe is preposterous in anyone's estimation. ALL of our internal problems would abate if we used those funds to feed our own hungry, provide excellent health care to our citizenry, build better roads and bridges, develop alternative energy solutions and on and on and on.

Why...we could have the most incredible defense system known the world over if we used a fraction of that bullion to protect ourselves from "evil-doers" that might consider messing with us!

From an entirely different perspective now:

Sit down with a translator and speak with an Iraqi mother and see which of the following she would prefer:

    A. That her son blow himself up before the age of 10
    B. Her son to become a productive member of a thriving community.

You know her answer would be B if allowed the chance to render her response; but that Iraqi woman is not entitled to her opinion - and because of the oppression under which she is ruled one must go to the root source of the issue, the Iraqi man.

As far as the world population is concerned, the number of active terrorists is relatively minute. With the technology at our disposal we have the ability to thwart virtually any attacks that might come our way, and we should be proud of that. But here's another viewpoint:

There can be no doubt that the proliferation of terrorism is exacerbated by our involvement and occupation of THEIR homeland. It is clear that we are unwanted occupants, yet we stay.

What do you suppose would happen if we just picked up our tanks and mortars and missiles and tents and left? If we all went home with the express purpose of doing what we can to make life better for ALL Americans?

Would the terrorists escalate their attacks on us?

It is doubtful - but if you go on the premise that they are planning around the clock to bring about another awful tragedy like that perpetrated against us on 9/11 you must also understand that our sensibilities have been tested, that we as a freedom and peace-loving nation (at least as far as the people not involved in the war machine are concerned) will never again drop our guard.

We CAN live in a somewhat Utopian society but it will take a concerted effort on the part of our government to make that happen. And it starts with bringing our troops home right now. Sadly, the power brokers and the lobbyists do not remotely echo our sentiments when they climb back up Capitol Hill to Congress – or we wouldn't have troops stationed all around the globe all the time.

To reinforce my point about occupation I've decided to reprint a major portion of the following article which was written by *Laurence M. Vance,* a freelance writer and an adjunct instructor in accounting and economics at Pensacola Junior College in Pensacola, FL. It is dated March 16, 2004, appeared in LewRockwell.com and is titled:

THE U. S. GLOBAL EMPIRE

There is a new empire in town, and its global presence is increasing every day.

The kingdom of Alexander the Great reached all the way to the borders of India. The Roman Empire controlled the Celtic regions of Northern Europe and all of the Hellenized states that bordered the Mediterranean. The Mongol Empire, which was the largest contiguous empire in history, stretched from Southeast Asia to Europe.

The Byzantine Empire spanned the years 395 to 1453. In the sixteenth century, the Ottoman Empire stretched from the Persian Gulf in the east to Hungary in the northwest; and from Egypt in the south to the Caucasus in the north. At the height of its dominion, the British Empire included almost a quarter of the world's population.

Nothing, however, compares to the U.S. global empire. What makes U.S. hegemony unique is that it consists, not of control over great land masses or population centers, but of a global presence unlike that of any other country in history.

The extent of the U.S. global empire is almost incalculable. The latest "Base Structure Report" of the Department of Defense states that the Department's physical assets consist of *"more than 600,000 individual buildings and structures, at more than 6,000 locations, on more than 30 million acres."*

The exact number of locations is then given as 6,702 — divided into large installations (115), medium installations (115), and small installations/locations (6,472). This classification can be deceiving, however, because installations are only classified as small if they have a Plant Replacement Value (PRV) of less than $800 million.

The number of countries that the United States has a presence in is staggering. According the U.S. Department of State's list of "Independent States of the World" there are 192 countries in the world, all of which, except Bhutan, Cuba, Iran, and North Korea, have diplomatic relations with the United States. All of these countries except one (Vatican City) are members of the United Nations. According to the Department of Defense publication, "Active Duty Military Personnel Strengths by Regional Area and by Country," ***the United States has troops in 135 countries***.

Here is the list:

Afghanistan	Finland	Niger
Albania	France	Nigeria
Algeria	Georgia	North Korea
Antigua	Germany	Norway
Argentina	Ghana	Oman
Australia	Greece	Pakistan
Austria	Guatemala	Paraguay
Azerbaijan	Guinea	Peru
Bahamas	Haiti	Philippines
Bahrain	Honduras	Poland
Bangladesh	Hungary	Portugal
Barbados	Iceland	Qatar
Belgium	India	Romania
Belize	Indonesia	Russia
Bolivia	Iraq	Saudi Arabia
Bosnia and	Ireland	Senegal
Herzegovina	Israel	Serbia and Montenegro
Botswana	Italy	Sierra Leone
Brazil	Jamaica	Singapore
Bulgaria	Japan	Slovenia
Burma	Jordan	Spain
Burundi	Kazakhstan	South Africa
Cambodia	Kenya	South Korea
	Kuwait	
	Kyrgyzstan	
	Laos	
	Latvia	

Cameroon
Canada
Chad
Chile
China
Colombia
Congo
Costa Rica
Cote D'Ivoire
Cuba
Cyprus
Czech Republic
Denmark
Djibouti
Dominican
Republic
East Timor
Ecuador
Egypt
El Salvador
Eritrea
Estonia
Ethiopia
Fiji

Lebanon
Liberia
Lithuania
Luxembourg
Macedonia
Madagascar
Malawi
Malaysia
Mali
Malta
Mexico
Mongolia
Morocco
Mozambique
Nepal
Netherlands
New Zealand
Nicaragua

Sri Lanka
Suriname
Sweden
Switzerland
Syria
Tanzania
Thailand
Togo
Trinidad and Tobago
Tunisia
Turkey
Turkmenistan
Uganda
Ukraine
United Arab Emirates
United Kingdom
Uruguay
Venezuela
Vietnam
Yemen
Zambia
Zimbabwe

This means that the United States has troops in 70 percent of the world's countries. The average American could probably not locate half of these 135 countries on a map.

Regular troop strength ranges from a low of 1 in Malawi to a high of 74,796 in Germany. At the time the most recent "Personnel Strengths" was released by the government (September 30, 2003), there were 183,002 troops deployed to Iraq, an unspecified number of which came from U.S. forces in Germany and Italy.

The total number of troops deployed abroad as of that date was 252,764, not including U.S. troops in Iraq from the United States. Total military personnel on September 30, 2003, was 1,434,377.

This means that 17.6 percent of U.S. military forces were deployed on foreign soil and certainly over 25 percent if U.S. troops in Iraq from the United States were included. **_But regardless of how many troops we have in each country, having troops in 135 countries is 135 countries too many._**

The U. S. global empire — an empire that Alexander the Great, Caesar Augustus, Genghis Khan, Suleiman the Magnificent, Justinian, and King George V would be proud of.

－－－－－

In late 2011, this report is seven years old! The above numbers have likely increased over that timeframe, even though the plan is to bring all the troops stationed in Iraq home by this year's winter holidays; as indicated in a statement issued by President Barack Obama from the White House on Friday, October 21, 2011.

Why do we need to be spread out like this? The countries we are occupying don't require our occupation. Seriously, we have 1 person in Malawi? What's the point? That 1 person is, however, a symbol; as he or she is the first of the total number of soldiers and civilians that should be on the next flight bound for home.

We can never have a perfect world, but this would be a fantastic start.

PS: Can ANYONE tell me where Malawi is?

DOCTOR OF DUNK

He's seven-foot four barely fits through the door
but he dribbles beyond comprehension

It's all just the same he can't spell his own name
and his salary's too BIG to mention.

Compare him to those with such menial roles
as the teachers who raise our poor youth.

This may sound sarcastic but brains of elastic
are stretching away at the truth.

Ten million a year makes the dunker with flash
while those with degrees stand in line.

What terminal fan controls the tall man
and determines the free-throw divine?

Racing down the court making money through sport
is probably not all that bad...

But make some restrictions; heed humble convictions
so our state of affairs won't turn sad.

Call these sour grapes but the vine often rapes
as it steals from the poor and oppressed...

Next time if you will evaluate skill
perhaps then we short people can rest!

RHYTHM, RHYME & SONG

I want to play like Horowitz and compose my very soul...
to caress the keyboard gingerly and take complete control.

Such strength in those two hands of his as they fly from key to
key...a more intense technician I doubt we'll ever see.

I want to write like Shakespeare and justify the word...
and have my sonnets picked apart and carefully observed.

A collection of my written works displayed for all to see...
a garden full of food for thought, a novel thought indeed.

I want to sing like Caruso with pitch beyond belief...
and scale right through three octaves without pausing for relief.

A chorus wrapped around one voice so powerfully complete...
to serenade in village squares, now that sounds really neat.

Perhaps such genius gathered in one room might sound surreal...
but imagine the respect I'd get, how humbled I would feel;

If they'd accept my invitation and join me for some tea...

Just Vladimir, Sir William, Enrico and Me!

BUT PATIENCE, DEAR DOCTOR

There's traffic jams and White House scams
or stepping down on nails;

There's too much noise from little boys
or getting dressed in tails.

There's overcharged, being caught off guard
or biting into bones;

There are high priced steaks and rotten breaks
or faulting on our loans.

There's cutting grass or flunking class
by staying out all night;

Poor sex lives, pimples and hives
or getting beat up in a fight.

But Patience, Dear Doctor…

I meant not to shock her,
but below are some reasons to weep:

There's no feeling of pride left deep down inside
for the man on the street anymore;

There's animosity, less generosity,
and no shelter called home for the poor.

Disease and affliction, a hard drug addiction
and puppies left out in the cold;

Wife beating fools who ignore all the rules
while victims leave stories untold.

Child abuse or being of no use
and running away in despair;

Those who will try to make out on the sly...
and neighbors who simply don't care.

Cigarette smoking or life without joking,
for humorless lives are in pain;

Observers who won't witness, poor physical fitness,
and strangers left out in the rain.

Prophets whose profits steal faith from our pockets
proclaiming the world will soon end;

Children without mothers or fathers or others
to honor or simply call "friend."

Unmotivated souls without any goals,
who claim that their chance never came.

So many things should be ruffling our wings...
like hatred, malpractice and shame.

THE KING IS IN HIS PENTHOUSE

The King is in his penthouse counting all OUR money;
we peasants thirty-six floors down don't really find him funny.

He stares into the sky and dreams of interest earned;
our kettle's boiling over and we're sick of getting burned.

What are we supposed to do and who are we to see;
when we think that we've been cheated
and our boss just won't agree?

We cannot boycott certain things like food, if we're to live;
but we can direct a protest at this mock-executive.

Let's bring down the corporate Prez at least a flight or two;
those stairs that separate us were built by me and you.

Did he forget the little man or how he got his start?
It's time our own best interests were taken more to heart.

WITHOUT WARNING

The old man gazes back at him as he stares into the mirror;
those wrinkles, once called laugh lines
are growing deep and clearer.

The hairline somehow disappeared, receding through the years;
his future looks uncertain as he fights away the tears.

A shirtless frame bears folds of flesh that once were bands of steel;
it seems that somewhere down the line he's lost his sex appeal.

He presses closer to look beyond the image now reflected;
the eyes of age and ages past see just what he expected:

How quickly life had passed him by
without the slightest warning...

It all seemed just like yesterday when he woke up this morning.

— — — — —

This one probably couldn't be any more autobiographical
than it is. Funny thing, though, I wrote it when I was in my mid
20's; when I allowed myself to be follicularly affected.

The mirror now reflects a man
with not a hair on top;
who's happy with the face he sees,
and *that* says quite a lot!

65

TELL ME TALES

Being as avid a fan as I am of man,
I'm curious why some choose to follow such rocky roads.

Tell me about destiny and all about fate,
and I'll show you freedom of choice and power to create.

Tell me your luck is all bad and your step's out of stride,
and I'll teach you to confront obstacles and conquer them.

Tell me you deserve a better life...just because,
and I'll prove to you how fine your situation already is.

Tell me you have limitations and goals unattainable,
and I'll point out pictures of man in flight.

Tell me that with a fuller purse you'd fare that much better,
and I'll insist that you study the life and times of Howard Hughes.

Tell me of talent and missing big breaks,
and I'll teach you to enjoy simple things,
like singing in the shower.

Tell me your voice should really be heard,
and I'll show you just how powerful actions can be.

Tell me of time and all you have left,
and I'll show you the baby robbed from its cradle.

Tell me what is on your mind and be sincere,
and I will be a friend to you forever.

I really am an avid fan,
of flowers and trees, of God and man.

SOFT-BOILED CANDIDATE

Egg us on and egg us on until the egg's on us;
promise us most anything to cultivate our trust.

Then take away our benefits and honor not our claim;
DECEPTION is the ruling force in our political game.

"I'll wipe away all poverty and clean our city's streets...
you'll hear a different drummer and dance to different beats!"

"Our children all will have the chance to live their brightest
dreams...your pride and joy will hardly keep
from bursting at the seams!"

Egg us on and egg some more as if you really care;
but the *yolk* of all your promises is much too hard to bear.

You've promised job security and taxes going down;
and equal rights with equal pay and streetlights lit downtown...

But all that you've delivered since we've made you our man;
were windy morning speeches that echoed your brave plan.

You said to vote Republican, that the Democrats all failed...
your party's ship flies half-mast now, its ship just never sailed.

— — — — —

I was going to spend a few pages ranting about our political system
but decided that if ever I wrote a poem that was self-explanatory,
this one was it. Therefore, on the subject...I'm done for a while.

PHYSICAL FIT

We let our bodies bite the dust at twenty-five or so
when most of us have fifty-five or sixty years to go.

We cram the goodies down our throats and ask for second portions
we get so fat - to just sit down, we go through massive contortions.

There's never time to exercise when the TV could be on
we prefer the feast to famine and that's our built-in con.

A sit-up in the morning is a horrifying sight
especially when chocolate chips were eaten late last night.

So the fatty tissue multiplies a little more each year
and when we think we've had enough
there's still some room...for fear!

Our hearts are taxed much more by us than by our Uncle Sam
and our legs are under pressure when all we do is stand.

So next time pass the kitchen and jog out to the yard
and work off some unwanted flesh...before it turns to lard.

UNTIL WE BECOME THE NEWS

The Eleven O' Clock News is serious stuff -
horrible events that happen daily.

A child is raped and murdered and they show us families
weeping in front of the camera...LIVE!

So we wait anxiously, poised for the Weather and Sports,
and it is impossible for us to realize what tragedy occurred -

until WE become the news.

The images fade quickly, out of sight and out of mind
and we remain forever removed from the truth -

Until WE become the news.

The pain and sorrow that tragedy brings are shut out.

Out of Fear?

Perhaps.

OR...

Out of Hope.

Hope that WE are never the ones shown on TV, LIVE...

Weeping.

NUCLEAR WASTE

It used to be the Joneses we'd try to keep up with.

Then it was the Russians...

No conspiratorial myth.

We used to try to drive a car the neighbors would admire;

Now we must build missiles and be prepared to FIRE!

We used to cut our lawns real short to keep them manicured.

Now we dig out silos, how maliciously absurd.

We used to walk to school each day and never had to fear.

Now the kids cut class and say "There may be NO next year!"

The pressing of a finger in anger or in haste
can totally obliterate our so called "human" race.

So much for the stockpiling and trying to keep pace;

For in the END no one will win -
cuz we'll ALL be nuclear waste.

DEAR DAD

You taught me right from wrong.

You pointed out roses among the thorns.

You taught me silent strength.

You showed me that it's okay for grown men to cry.

You showed me that *there are no failures,*
only stepping stones to success.

You taught me honesty and integrity in business.

You are my idol.

You are my hero.

You are my friend.

I wanted you to know this now...so you can feel my love for you
as we both grow older, wiser and closer.

I only hope that I can someday be the kind of father to my son
that you have been to me.

I Love You, Dad

THE MIRACLE CALLED DARREN
(a 4-part chronological series)

Someone Inside

God!
It's amazing.

A Miracle.
I can feel it reaching out to touch my hands placed on your tummy.

We DID it!

Just you and I
no outside help
or suggestions
or anything.

Just you and I and nobody else.

I wish,

I really wish

I could see it NOW!

Waiting three more months is out of the question.

My patience will never last.
All the parts are there already.

Moving.

Growing…

...calling out to you and me and the world it will soon greet.

How about one tiny peek?

Please?

Pretty please with a cherry on top,
with whipped cream
and four scoops of chocolate ice cream and...

Alright, I'll wait.

Let's see...

Only 90 days left.

89, 88, 87...

One of my favorite stories I like to tell was the time when we went for a sonogram; THE sonogram that would reveal our child's sex. Being all "cool" I told my wife that it was alright for her to know if she wants, but I'd rather be surprised on the day the child is born. And, "no matter what" don't tell me if you know.

On the way home from the pediatrician's office I knew she knew. I was still cool for about 4 miles, when finally I had to know. "Okay" I said "go ahead and tell me."

Holding me to my insistence she refused to discuss the subject. I had no alternative than to stop at the next traffic light, get out of the car and say "I'm not coming back in until you tell me!" I proceeded to lie down under the front end of the vehicle until she spilled it; smiling and utterly boasting "Alright, alright...I don't know whether we should get it a baseball glove or a football helmet!" After crying like a baby, I thought...not only was I going to be a daddy, I was going to have a son!

SOMETIMES I WONDER

I wonder if every new parent is so amazed,
so aglow with the excitement of having their first child.

I wonder what color his eyes will finally be
what roads he'll turn down
and what kind of friend he'll turn out to be.

I wonder if he'll ever know how complete he has made my life
and if we'll be best buddies someday.

I wonder how long it will take him to learn his ABC's, to tie his
shoes and if he'll use one bow or two, or leave them in knots.

I wonder if he will keep his uninhibited outlook on life
long enough to share it with others
and if he'll hang on to a strong sense of humor
in times of trouble.

I wonder if he'll dance to the beat of a different drummer,
if he'll carry a tune or share his toys.

I wonder if he'll be affected by discrimination
or if he'll rise above such common intolerances.

I wonder if he'll be six foot four or five foot nine
and if he'll visit me when I grow old.

I wonder if he'll ever hesitate to talk to me when he needs me
or if he'll be able to confide in me always.

I wonder if he'll speak admirably of his parents
when he's with his friends
and if he'll eat green vegetables.

I wonder if he'll be able to heal himself in body and spirit
and if his touch will warm the hearts of others.

I wonder if he'll settle down someday and get married
and brag about our grandchildren getting new teeth.

I wonder if he'll get the chance to travel
and explore the roots of his ancestors
or if he'll take an interest in extra sensory perception.

But even as I wonder about these things
I can't help thinking that no matter
what he decides to do with his life
it will be just fine by me...

Because he is my little baby boy.

Sometimes I wonder...but deep down inside, I know!

WELL, LET'S SEE

His eyes are brilliantly brown. Not one road he's traveled has been perilous to date. We are as emotionally close as a father and son can be, though there is pain in being separated by so many miles.

I don't remember how long it took him to learn his ABC's but he knew every Matchbox car that was ever built by the time he was 2½, including the 1937 Duesenberg or Duesy as he and other enthusiasts of the vehicle more commonly referred to it.

He knew the species name of every dinosaur that roamed the planet by the time he was three!

I'll never forget when he politely corrected the curator of a children's museum; saying "Excuse me, Sir...Sir! It's no longer called a Brontosaurus, it's an Apatosaurus; they "extinced" the other name a few years ago." And he was RIGHT!

He eats everything, doesn't matter the color or if it is a vegetable.

He hasn't a bigoted bone in his body.

He is nearly six feet tall with the full head of hair that his father never viewed in the mirror.

He isn't afraid to take calculated risks.

He is stubborn in a positive way.

He will fight for what he believes in.

He is the most loyal person I've ever met.

He has a quiet confidence in himself and trusts his instincts.

He is a pet lover.

He is a sports lover.

He is a people lover.

He isn't afraid to question authority.

He dares to go against the grain.

He is poetic.

He is respectful.

He is colorful.

He is a talker.

He is a looker.

He is a doer,

He is intelligent...

Receiving several academic scholarships to one of the best Schools of Journalism in America, he did it all while being popular, never nerdy, a great friend to many and dancing to his own beat while sharing his heart...as well as his toys!

He is sensitive, non-judgmental, pensive, thoughtful, and true to himself.

He is classy.

He is brassy.

He is bold.

He is sincere.

He's done some traveling.

He WILL get married some day.

He will be a real catch, that's for sure.

He will be successful in business.

He will be an asset to the human race.

He has never ended a phone conversation with words other than "I love you, Dad!"

He is my pride, my joy and the greatest gift to my beating heart.

He will forever be a source of light in my life.

I was right, wasn't I?

Deep down inside...I knew!

He is, and will always be...

My little baby boy!

WAY TOO FAST FORWARD

I sit at a computer that was unheard of back then, entering poetry on my own website.

Such are the advancements we've made.

And as I pause to reflect on the previous poem I am simply overwhelmed to the core.

The first offering in this 4-part series was written on February 20, 1983.

It is now June 21, 2006.

That dream, that fascination, that gift, that life is now 23!

Darren graduated from college last month.

And while I knew the time would someday come -

Boy, did it get here quickly.

WAY TOO FAST FORWARD, indeed.

It is humbling to age.

It is frightening too.

It is remarkable.

It is a blessing.

I embrace it.

I marvel at it.

I am enriched by it.

And my hope and prayer for the future is that my son can feel the same sense of joy that I do; the joy that comes as a result of being a father to a wonderful child.

I hope he lives his life to the fullest and that he derives joy from *most* everything he does.

I say *most*, because there truly is much to be derived from the minor cracks and crevices along our journey; and if he experiences no setbacks he'll not learn the value of fighting the good fight...and prevailing.

Man, 23 years.

Time sure does fly by.

Amazing!

UPDATE:

And now he's nearly 29. A Masters Degree has been added to his solid résumé and I believe he's found true love in his life. Beaming, glowing, thrilled, excited and thoroughly fulfilled are minor adjectives to describe my feelings for this truly beautiful human being and how it is all turning out for him.

DIVINE PERCEPTIONS

In our deepest, darkest moments of despair
when we're not so sure if anyone is there...

In those lonely, silent hours of the night
when our mortal souls are overcome with fright...

In split second meditation
when the subject is creation...

In the quiet of our dreams
when we've put to rest our schemes...

When all else seems to fail
and we're rendered weak and frail...

We Find God.

But when we violate commandments
by not honoring our parents...

When we harm our own existence
buy cocaine or bare false witness...

When we're searching for brass rings
and materialistic things...

When we're jealous of a stranger
or refuse someone in danger...

When we kill our fellow man
In Iraq or Pakistan...

We've Lost God!

BROKEN BARRIERS

What's all this news about Christians or Jews?

What difference does it make, I'm looking for clues?

Too many alternatives tend to confuse,

It's not cut and dried and not win or lose.

So...

Break down the barriers and sing not the blues;

Join hands together and extinguish that fuse.

WHY BUY AT ALL?

They attack at our intelligence and brainwash all our minds,
they think we'll buy their products as Christmas time unwinds.

But who could they be kidding when they say their brand is better,
and why should Spot eat Alpo if he's an English setter?

Why buy burgers from "The King"
when all ground beef's the same?

And why should Klein's caress our buns,
who said "What's in a name?"

You can't convince the average Joe one shave cream beats another
or that "This car is just for you...go borrow from your brother!"

For every item there's a list of ten competitors
and while they boast that one's the best...

Why is it NEVER yours?

Their cutthroat advertisements all claim a closer shave
but the blade cuts so much closer...

Since their road of doubt's been paved.

DAYTIME TRAUMA

When last we met in Soapy Town,
Alexis spilled coffee on Tara's new gown…

And Joshua shot at his long-lost flame
just because she forgot his last name.

The police inspector was caught in bed
conducting improper inspections instead.

Jessica's pregnant with no husband in sight
she just can't remember who she slept with that night!

The patient, Jeffrey in 423
came in with a cold and they lopped off his knee.

Dr. Johnson proclaimed that one knee was enough
for Jeffrey - swallowing that news was pretty tough.

Rachel has trouble maintaining control
she's marrying Eric who's out on parole.

The poison that Ashley mixed into Dale's drink
is still in his glass and it's starting to stink.

Megan had a facelift and liver spots removed
if only she could have her personality improved.

Rex was hustling hookers in faded old blue jeans
but the ladies hustled off in long black limousines.

John changed his name to Daphne in court
claiming the operation was his only resort.

Rita is breaking it off with her man
22 years was all she could stand.

Where will it all end, what's next to go down?
Tune in tomorrow for more "Soapy Town!"

RIOT-TORN & WONDERING

The city streets are crying at the damage that's been done,
the riot-torn inferno wages battles never won.

The depraved now band together but cannot organize,
breaking out in all directions, shaking fists against the skies.

What has turned them toward the street in anger and in rage?
Don't they sense the curtain crashing down upon their stage?

They've set afire the very roots that lead to their distinction,
but the matches struck that moonlit night
could lead them to extinction.

The timid souls in growing boys convince them to take part,
but when the ashes finally clear, they find no place to start.

The younger children wonder as they watch them do their thing...
has the evil deep inside them condoned this vicious fling?

Yes, the city streets are crying at the damage and the pain
as the riot-torn inferno lies smoldering in the rain.

GOOSE BUMPS

If MUSIC is the sound of life
then symphony is grand.

If MUSIC sparks the deadest soul
the melody's in demand.

If MUSIC stands our skin on end
and goose bumps travel through...

Then writing songs for all to hear is what we ought to do.

If MUSIC fills the background
and other sounds just noise...

Then drop that platinum CD in and listen to its joys.

If MUSIC is the champion that wins a heart or two
then play for me eternally...

A song that's rich and true.

MOVIE MADNESS

Pictures in motion

a film-maker's potion

for bringing to life childhood dreams...

Like sailing the ocean

or betting a notion

and winning it all, so it seems.

Of being a hero

or ruling like Nero

and landing in jail for your schemes.

Intrigue and suspense

Black-Belt self defense,

such are the cinema's themes.

Of conquering nations

without limitations

achievements without a delay.

Beautiful faces

and winning all races

my, what a brilliant display.

Of master disguises

no one realizes,

leading ladies that beg you to stay.

Of slaying the dragons

or circling the wagons;

adventure your breath takes away.

Now these are the dreams

that light up silver screens

and help us escape for the day.

URGENT BULLETIN!

We have...

telephones

radios

satellites

typewriters

keyboards

books

letters

songs

headphones

newspapers

sign language

body language

computers

hearing aids

the Internet

walkie-talkies

video

audio

wire services

reporters

public speakers

news anchors

translators

recording devices

speech therapists

politicians

magazines

libraries

meetings

committees

action groups

networking

conference calls

So...

…why is it so difficult for people
to communicate with one another?

THE THINGS I LIKE

I like the rain, except on Saturday nights
before a Sunday morning softball game.

I like men who aren't afraid to cry and
adults that aren't afraid to act like children.

I like dining out or eating in and dressing up
or wearing ratty old T-Shirts.

I like touching, kissing, music and ice-cold watermelon.

I like wine and cheese with real close friends
and small-talking with strangers.

I like couples that brag about their spouses
and Original Recipe KFC.

I like winters in the South and summers anywhere,
and the smell of burning leaves.

I like pine trees, freshly mown lawns
and families that stick together.

I like double-stuffed Oreos and poetry that
really and truly touches the heart.

I like young, healthy bodies lying in the sand
and suntans that never seem to fade.

I like dreaming in Technicolor and the winter holidays.

I like girls who ask out boys
and opening vacuum-packed jars.

I like anyone who knows how to play the piano
and the lines etched in the faces of the elderly.

I like holding my breath under water and
watching Monday Night Football with my Dad...

NOT necessarily at the same time!

I like masquerade parties that don't just
take place on Halloween night.

I like watching people read my poetry - to see if
I can sense their interpretation through their body language.

I like funny movies and fireworks and
fresh, home-grown fruits and veggies.

I like the dark and how it forces me to contemplate
the day's past events and envision the next morning.

I like professional athletes who
give back to their communities.

I like anyone who donates their time, energy,
influence or money to help others.

I like people who care enough
to work with the Special Olympics.

I like BBQ-ing and sleeping a whole day away
if I feel like it.

I like people with abundant knowledge
and sufficient patience to share some of it.

I like completing challenging projects
and helping friends move.

I like giving presents, because doing so
makes everyone happy, especially ME!

I like romantic dinners, taking in a ballgame at the park,
just hanging out with a few friends…and pretty much
everything you like.

And I like to write them down.

WITH BLINDERS ON

Wrath and indignation are the talk around the nation,
Justice and its virtues...damn near eradication.

The halls of schools all reek with sweat,
and not from students bearing down on books they haven't read.

The sweat we smell is body heat...of boys chased down the halls,
and the smoke is not from cigarettes...like Winston or Pall Malls.

So, where to turn at 3PM when their parents aren't at home?
Out to the streets with the gangs and the geeks
is where they'll likely roam.

Just what could they be looking for and what could be in store,
but bars and cots and three square meals...
who could ask for anything more?

The private sector looks away, erasing any doubt
that they have some idea of what the real world's all about.

But that old asphalt jungle can house in one small cage,
the anger of all urban blight, the noxious fumes of rage.

Tune in to the evening news with Harry and the boys,
a raping here, a killing there, and so much godless noise.

Articulated pointers on how to do the same;
so watch us very carefully...
then go outside and play!

FREE ADVICE

Don't throw it away!

Poems are like pictures, they capture thoughts
and fleeting moments.

So what if your poetry doesn't always rhyme
and your stories are predictable...

Don't throw them away!

Share with us what is on your mind;
let us learn from what you write.

Don't deprive us of what is so important these days...
the written word.

We can interpret them any way we choose.

We can assume...

We can complain...

We can worry...

We can be forced to think...

We can enjoy...

We can dream...

We can wish we'd said that...

We can feel what you felt when you penned it!

But please, don't cap your pen and go back to your nine to five.

We all will miss out, including you;
for you will never know how we feel about your writing,
and you will never know what it means
to touch someone with words
unless you share what you've written with us.

Keep off the cap...
and let your words continue to flow.

We will all be better for it.

Too many of us conceal our deepest, proudest thoughts
behind a wall of doubt and our inspirational moments
lie dormant at a time when all mankind could benefit.

YOU CAN QUOTE ME ON THAT
(UNLESS OTHERWISE ATTRIBUTED)

"Dance like you hired the band. Sing like you wrote the song. Share joy as if it's all you know. Then go live the dreams you dare to imagine."

"Life would be so much clearer if every sign could be as easily understood as WET PAINT!"

"Love is the currency of life. It is accepted everywhere!"

"You cannot paint with an empty palette. Your dreams are your colors; let your actions be your brushes."

"NEVER stop trying. It is that perseverance that will land you in the arena of your dreams. Once there, make a difference."

"If at first you don't succeed, your preparation was wrong."

"If copper is 25¢ per ounce, does that make 25 pennies more valuable than a quarter?"

"Never fish for compliments when you feel unappreciated, you probably won't get them then either!"

"Take time to smell the roses, but carry insect repellant, just in case."

"It doesn't make sense to take our senses for granted."

"Video games were invented to take our minds off reality. Now, they are our reality!"

"You don't have to be mindless to watch television, but it helps."

"Do something different today, but don't brag about it tomorrow or you'll be just like everyone else."

"I always root for the underdog, but rarely put money on him."

"Failure is a four-letter word. Actually fail is a four-letter word, but you get what I mean."

"We are all victims or victors based on our own interpretations!"

"When you doubt, you lose - if nothing more than the courage to continue!"

"If it didn't start out green and it is now, throw it out!"

"I once had a great idea about how to get out of prison; but it escapes me now."

"Stop worrying about your health and start worrying about everything else that is bothering you right now."

"Albert Einstein once said that the hardest thing in the world to understand is the income tax. If that's the case, how in the world are the rest of us morons supposed to get it?"

"The surest sign that intelligent life exists elsewhere in the universe is the green, glowing, cigar-shaped object hovering over my house at the moment!"

"The single most important characteristic is honesty; even when it hurts."

"The most productive word in the entire universe is also one of its smallest; TRY."

"The most destructive word in the entire universe is also one of its smallest;   LIE."

"The final word in the universe is also one of its smallest; DIE."

"Today is tomorrow's once upon a time. Make your history happy!"

"There are no failures, only stepping stones to success!"
(I know it's on pages 30 & 71 - but it's worth repeating a couple of times, don't you think?)

"Why should any person require more than one washcloth in their lifetime?"

"A bald man never underestimates the year-round value of a hat."

"I'd rather be afraid of the dark than the light."

"Procrastination is like staring at a clock that you know has no batteries and still expecting it to keep the proper time."

"Even a blind acorn finds a squirrel once in a while."

"I had this dream - that money didn't really matter much. When I woke up I couldn't buy friendship, I couldn't buy love and I couldn't buy health. Perhaps I wasn't dreaming at all."

"What happens if you live to do everything on your bucket list?"

"If you were addicted to taking money out of your bank and could no longer do it, would you suffer withdrawal withdrawals?"

"The only thing constant about change is that it no longer buys you a cup of coffee."

"I think it's possible to be happy wherever you happen to be. More state of mind than State in which you live."

"When you're feeling down, look up. When you're feeling up, don't look down!"

"I don't have a lot of money lying around, but I'm richer than I've ever been. That's MY spiritual estimation of fulfillment."

"I got out of bed on the wrong side this morning and spent an hour thinking we remodeled the closet to look like the living room."

"The reward for seeing a job through to its completion is confidence to attempt another."

"Make you a deal, Son. I won't take credit for things you do right as long as you don't blame me for the things you do wrong."
~ *Carole Ann Rothman Perry*
(April 26, 1934 – August 17, 1989 – always Mom)

"Watch out, Mister! You're going to wind up in the Lebitsonian Institute one of these days if you keep that up!"
~ *Ada Walt* (Momm)

"You've got the talent to do anything in the world you want to do. Don't let anyone keep you from achieving your dreams!"
~ *Paul H. Perry* (Dad)

"God doesn't need salespeople."
~ Judy Perry (Soul Mate)

"Know what happens when you don't do anything or go anywhere? Nothing!"
~ Rolland Walt (Dadd)

"As a waiter, I often wonder why someone believes you when you tell them there are ten billion stars in the sky, but have to check when you say… **Be careful, this plate is extremely HOT!"**

"Going to church doesn't make you a Christian any more than standing in a garage makes you a car!"
~ Laurence Peter

"It's all about YOU, isn't it?"
~ Nina Lynn Harmelin (Sister)

"He's even got the nerve to talk behind his own back."

"Find out what gives you the most joy doing and do it even if it means not taking home a paycheck for it. The payback will be tenfold without the money."

"I made a terrible mistake one time and thought I was mistaken. Sure am glad I realized it in time; and I'll try not to let it happen again!"

"The end always mustifies the jeans!"
~ Zachary Adam Perry (Brother -The BEST
spoonerism of all time!)

*"If all the world's a stage, where does
the audience sit?"*

*"My guess is if she knew we were
making money selling the natural
resources that she gave us free of
charge, Mother Nature would be
extremely perturbed?"*

To that point:

Evian, the packaged water, spelled backward is **Naïve**."

*"Do you think you'd read **more** or **less**
once you find out how many trees have
to die to build a single library?"*

"Wouldn't it be safer if politicians walked instead of ran for office?"

"We have two ears and one mouth so we can hear what we are eating!"

"I played a game of chess against myself today. I won and I suppose I lost. Does that mean I'm really good or really bad at chess?

"Hope is the ability to hear the music of the future. Faith is having the courage to dance to it today."

~ Daniella Cappelli

I never met Daniella in person. Ours was a Facebook friendship that she initiated from her hospital room. I followed her brave battle with cancer online until her passing on October 11, 2010.

The above is a mere sampling of her regularly thought-provoking posts. I share it with you in her honor and in loving memory.

She died so young, was so beautiful, and is so deeply missed by so many; especially her lifelong BFF, Kellie DiPalma – now putting up the fight of her life against the same dread disease.

"Constructive criticism can have a demolishing effect."

"You call this a recession? Have you seen my hairline lately? That's an utter depression."

"How come you never dedicate any of your performances to me? I come to all of your shows!"
~ Harriet Israel (Family & Friend)

Well, Harriet, at least you were quoted in my second book!

"I stopped to smell the roses and got stung on the nose by a bee. Whose idea was that anyway, Honey?"

"The definition of irony: Being woken up by your alarm clock radio to Simon & Garfunkel's **The Sound of Silence!**"

"Live today like it was yesterday and know what it is like to tread water."

"The heart beats louder when money is at stake."

"Wealth is in the wallet of the beholder."

"Cancer is God's answer to a civilization that thinks it is perfect."

"The perfect balance would be for government to stay out of our bedrooms and out of our bank accounts."

"Riches are attainable but rarely ordainable."

"Teach a man to fish and he'll eat for a lifetime; Teach a man to drive a car and he'll probably drive to a lake and go fishing."

"If you truly love someone, try to leave their name off the mortgage; because a mortgage can be foreclosed upon - and love should remain open forever!"

"Dare to dream, but resist great risk."

"How long will it take man to realize his insignificance within our singular solar system?"

"Faith is believing that something invisible will break our fall."

"Strength is getting back up after we fall and not being afraid to start all over again."

"I'd rather run out of money than time."

"The notion that anyone lives a long time is preposterous in the grand scheme of things."

"A burning fire on a cold winter night feels better than any air-conditioned room on a hot summer night."

"Poor Richard was right. A penny saved IS a penny earned; which means if you save a penny every day for 80 years you'll have $292.00. WOW!"

"Illegal aliens are ruining this country; always double-parking their spaceships like that!"

"What we need is the strength to cure our weaknesses and the humility to know we still have a long way to go."

"The flames of justice are but smoldering embers to those who have been betrayed by the legal system."

"Richness is a term for dessert, not a measure of a person's true value."

"When those around me are upset; I'm more inclined to think it's because they are confused - rather than believing their anger stems from something I've actually done wrong."

"Peace in the world will only come when organized religion loosens its vice-like grip on its inhabitants."

"A man can stand tall in the face of adversity, but that doesn't necessarily make him a tall man."

"You can find more happiness by sharing a sense of humor than you can by sharing a wallet full of cash."

*"A manufacturing **plant** can only grow if its **seeds**, the employees, are willing to work hard to make it **sow**."*

"Water a flower and it grows. Water the lawn and it grows. Pour water on an oil fire and it too grows."

"I went outside into the bright sunlight...then it dawned on me."

"Trying to spread peace is a lot like trying to spread marmalade. As is the case with the bread, there's always a part of the world that doesn't hold kindly to it?"

"There's one thing that you can change about yourself immediately, and that's your attitude."

"Out of inspiration and through perspiration completion is achieved."

"He is flakier than any box of cereal on the shelves."

"When doubt enters the picture, that's the time our mettle is tested most."

"Fear is nothing but the inability to be at peace with our decisions."

*"**Driving** up the price of oil? Do they have to use **that** verb?"*

"A gift is only truly treasured by the recipient when it is given from the heart; unless, it's a 70"Hi-Def, 3-D TV with brilliant Surround Sound."

"Where there's a will there's a way...to get the surviving family members quarreling."

"Chain letters are as valuable as a mostly-charred treasure map."

"It is better to discuss something than live in disgust over it."

"He was as skinny as a matchstick and just as hot headed."

"A short temper is something that can get the best of you while taking the most out of you."

"He wore suspenders so people would think he lost a lot of weight."

"Drinking is never a problem as long as it's water from a glass."

"The choice of any nation to go to war or stay home and improve life within their own borders seems to be a simple one."

"Failing to quit trying isn't failure either."

"Never trust people who share the secrets of their success with you; it only proves one thing... they can't keep a secret."

"When a person begins a sentence with the words **'To tell you the truth'** *or* **'To be honest with you'** *- it makes me wonder if it's the first time that they are."*

"Everyone should have basic plumbing skills. That way when something goes down the wrong pipe, they'll know what to do."

"Meditation does for the soul what sunlight does for the disposition."

"A dinner without wine is like a day without sunshine."
~ Nerio Lelli

"Appreciate the days behind you for they may have been the best times you'll ever know."

"Rest assured that if you get enough sleep you'll rest assured."

"It's a good thing bakers can't count. I like their dozen."

"No matter how much money you have, you can't buy time."

"Keeping track of some peoples' ramblings is harder than counting grains of sand as they run out of an egg timer."

"The other day I called my boss to tell him I wasn't going to make it in to the office today because I had to attend my great grandmother's funeral again."

"In the eyes of a gold-digger, a man is only as tall as the wallet upon which he stands."

"If you have peace in your heart and love in your life - you have every human asset necessary."

"Running through puddles, dancing in the rain - are both pretty stupid if you can avoid them."

"Romance is not wiping off the lipstick after a kiss. Love is not needing lipstick **to** *kiss."*

"Legal briefs are the same as underwear briefs in that they hope to cover just about everything."

"When thoughts don't come and you become anxious while you're writing, read a collection of quotes. It's amazing how quickly you'll get back on track."

"I cannot praise the people who put their lives on the line to serve and protect us enough. That kind of unparalleled devotion to a career and to the human race is something that few of us are willing to or dare perform."

"The truth of the matter is that if we always knew the right thing to do and did it, the world would be a perfect place...and we couldn't possibly have THAT!"

"Paying your creditors off in full is better than sex; although I hope it happens less frequently for you."

"If you take two and two and add them together and don't get four perhaps you should become a baker."

"It would be ironic if while playing 'Hail to the Chief' at the presidential inauguration it actually started hailing."

"A significant part of life is spent waiting in line at the bathroom; more so if you're a female of the species."

"All the technological gadgetry today cannot replace the thrill of listening to a ballgame late at night with a transistor radio under your pillow."

"It is easier to interpret Shakespeare than it is to complete a project whose manual begins with the words - **Some Assembly Required***!"*

"If you leave fruit out in the sun and it grows, why doesn't the same thing happen to people from the same exposure?"

"I used to be bashful and shy. Now I'm timid and reluctant."

"They **appraised** *my house last year and it was worth less than it was when I bought it. Would it have made a difference if they* **praised** *it instead?"*

"Living in America is still better than living anywhere else in the world."

(That's it - that's the whole quote.)

"You can conquer all of your inner demons by believing in the good that will replace them."

"Political correctness is an oxymoron that should be banned forever. The notion that something is only correct when it is deemed so by a purported authority figure is as laughable as organized religion."

"The quickest way to wealth is through inheritance!"

"I never metaphor I didn't like."

"In this so-called human race we all end up at the same Finish Line."

(Unless you live in Finland - then it's the Finnish Line)

"It is better to be productive with your time than to write about it; unless you intend on publishing it."

"Racecar drivers must all be Democrats since their entire workday is spent turning left."

"In the mad dash to glory, man needs stumble only once to regain his humility."

"Fiscal fitness is just as important as physical fitness."

"He took a leap of faith and was instantly eaten by a shark."

"The real crux of the problem is the real crux of the problem."

"He said I could trust him, that he'd never stab me in the ba..."

"She's the kind of person that would call to you for help while drowning and then stand on top of your head to stay afloat."
~ Judy Perry (Soul Mate)

"I made a note to myself to write more notes to myself."

"Stupid is not a word that should be used excessively. That would be stupid."

"Don't be lazy. Always try to figure it out for yourself first."
~ Carole A. Perry (Mom, again!)

"Acupuncture is such a benign word for stabbing a person all over their body with very long needles."

"Redundancy happens over and over again with such constant repetition and frequency that it often gets overstated too many times and becomes totally redundant."

"He was so far down the depth chart they needed miners to get him out of the dugout."

"You can easily gauge a person's intelligence by the way he rights."

"YouTube has single-handedly taken the joy out of making an idiot out of oneself. Insanity that can be instantly viewed like that used to be reserved strictly for family members at the holiday dinner table."

"Much like hitting a 100mph fastball, the art of diplomacy is a developed skill."

"People need to listen more."

"Waiting for a bus to take me to pick up my car from my mechanic made me wonder why I didn't just buy a bus in the first place."

"Natural foods are humanity's greatest preservative."

"Follow your dreams, but if they end up looking like they belong to someone else, perhaps they weren't yours in the first place."

"Life is what you make it. Destiny is not the sole ruling force that determines your future."

"Tenderness is often best received by the toughest people."

"Sometimes taking the wrong turn turns out to be right."

"Unlike humans, trees are remarkable for knowing exactly when it's time for their leaves to change color."

"To be perfectly frank, it's time you were perfectly frank."

"He wore reflective sunglasses so that people could see exactly what he was seeing when he looked at them."

"Pressure is not facing a 0-2 count with the bases loaded in the bottom of the 9th inning down two runs. Pressure is working three jobs to try to make ends meet in order to put some bread on the table."

"I've never understood the preacher or rabbi who complains about the congregation's poor attendance while delivering their sermons to those attendees."

"I believe in the supreme power... of being ones self."

"Every minute that ever passes was the future only 60 seconds ago."

"It is no more human nature to give up than it is to persevere."

"When those around you fail to live up to their end of the bargain, yell foul!"

*"The answer to any question that starts out with...**what's the difference between** is...more vegetables! At least it is when I call for take-out at The China Inn."*

"The agitated driver shot a fellow commuter because he mistook getting the peace sign for being flipped off."

"The profits of prophets should be spiritual; not monetary."

"The pattern of life is simple. You are born, you go to school, you go to work and you go to...well, that's where it can get a bit confusing."

*"Have **you** ever gotten in the shorter and faster line at the bank or grocery store?"*

*"The father was such a **brilliant** actor his **sun** was impressed."*

"Make music or blueberry pancakes, not war!"

"Stop me if you've heard this quote before."

"If they replaced ignorance with tolerance everyone would lead a happier life."

"It should be - to the victor go the fresh; not the spoils."

"There are two things I want to do before I die; ride in a blimp and on a Zamboni."
~ Judy Perry (And perhaps you shall, princhipesa!)

"By natural process a family can multiply through addition; and that's a plus."

"No one has really spent time watching grass grow, have they?"

"My flagging vision causes me to take more time to see things for what they really are."

"In the blink of an eye, it is gone. So fragile and temporary is this thing called life."

"One of these days I'd like to read your poetry in a book!"
~ *Dad* (Well, here you go, Sir!)

"Life's too short, no matter how long you've got, so you might as well enjoy it!"
~ *Mom*
(Pretty much her last words and perfect for the last quote!)

HAPPIER NEW YEAR

Americans!
We are fighters.
We just LOVE to fight!
We fight to preserve peace.
We fight a drug war that cannot be won.
We fight against poverty,
but refuse to lift up the impoverished.
We fight to keep our freedom
but shoot innocent folks at peace rallies.
We fight to keep from losing our homes
but forget to make mortgage payments.
Maybe it's time to put down our guns and our fists.
Maybe it's time to set aside petty jealousy.
Maybe it's time to set aside our anger
and consider the consequences
before raging onward.
This year let's try something different.
This year let's try to spread rampant joy.
This year let's work to balance our moral compasses.
This year let's not fight each other over everything.
This year let's see what we can do
to make the world a more peaceful place.
If we are unsuccessful in our attempts
we can confidently say…

At least we fought for it!

HOW TO FIX AMERICA

(A 12-Step Program)

1. Eliminate federal, state and local income tax entirely. Once this is accomplished there cannot be any cheating. The rich will get richer, but so will the middle class and less privileged. By eliminating income tax, Americans will have infinitely more spending power from top to bottom, which will boost the GNP effective immediately.

2. Implement an across-the-board sales tax of 15% on all American-made products and 25% on all foreign-produced products, including food, automobiles, etc. This will encourage purchasing products made by our citizens that are no longer inferior to those produced outside of America - because the funding will be there for paying employees a just and fair wage, and will still allow for importing. This will ensure major corporations the ability to proliferate their profit-making by virtue of not having to concern themselves with "sheltering" or "loop-holing" or employing various other "sneaky" tactics in order to keep more of their money. They can still buy all their big, expensive toys - and the government will benefit by the sales tax paid on them.

3.	The minimum wage for all jobs needs to be increased to $15.00 an hour. Prices of goods will necessarily increase, but the lack of paying income tax will offset those increases in plausible fashion. For example: If restaurants are paying a minimum of $15 an hour to all employees, including wait staffs, line cooks, dishwashers, etc. this will necessarily drive up food costs and operational expenses, however, by not paying any taxes other than the assessed sales tax on the back end for the food they provide their diners, their overall revenue will increase, not decrease.

4.	Charge a flat rate import tariff of 20% to all manufacturers shipping goods to the United States.

5.	Pull all troops out of all foreign countries regardless of their purpose for being there; thereby instantly bringing trillions of dollars to America for the purpose of improving our own infrastructure; building roads, rail & other mass transit systems, solar energy plants, schools, etc. At the same time this will pave the way for deeper grants in the technology and research sectors and create millions of jobs for our citizens. Outsourcing won't be necessary. We won't have to send American civilians to the Middle East for high paying jobs or have to worry about subjecting them to the inherent dangers of that region.

6.	Maintain a strong defense force here at home, while paying soldiers the same salaries they received overseas. That will immediately employ thousands of hard-working Americans that we know are interested in preserving our freedom by protecting our shores. Special Forces will be kept here at home and be highly paid for their capabilities; the only difference is the "War Machine" will be dismantled and its equipment maintained and protected on our shores - to be quickly dusted off in the event our nation is under attack. However, our nation will not be under attack from other countries once we stop our worldwide meddling and insistence of spreading peace throughout the world by might and self-appointment. The United States will not have to worry about defending Israel, as Israel, if any nation has the market cornered on security and self-preservation as a means of survival since it became a State in 1948. Let us learn from this ally as they work to perfect airport security in a non-discriminatory fashion. A fantastic system that is almost ready to implement and makes total sense is a booth through which all passengers must pass *with* their carry-on luggage. Other than the customary size restrictions, there is no limitation to what passengers may bring into the booth with them, but here's the caveat: ***This security booth is programmed to detonate any explosives immediately upon detection.*** This would mean the end of racial profiling, the end of wondering how many ounces of toothpaste a 95 year old woman can take onboard with her...and if a terrorist disguised as a 95 year old wants to whip out a pair of knitting needles and threaten to take down her plane, bring it on, baby!

7. The United States government will provide health care, including emergency surgeries and extended care to its citizens without question. This can be done by establishing what I call the WHAT IF fund - to be disseminated among the health care facilities throughout the country on a

computed scale commensurate with the surgical procedures of patients on a case by case basis, adding humanity back into the picture. **WHAT IF** being the acronym for the: **W**e **H**ave **A**mple **T**echnology **I**nfrastructure **F**und that will be readily available once all American troops return home.

8. Cut matching payroll taxes out completely for all small businesses and in half for medium to large businesses. This eases the burden for small business that will now have to pay the $15 per hour minimum wage. It will not effect middle to large business; however, they will still get the 50% tax break.

9. Provide college education to every child in America that wants it, period. On a clearly thought out sliding scale make certain that teachers' salaries are in line with their achieved status, with a starting salary comparable to technical and other 4-year college degree earned positions.

10. Cap insurance company premium rates based on factoring the income earning ability of its customers; taking into consideration previous Auto, Home and Life scenarios. For excellent drivers, reduce auto insurance rates across the board. For generally healthy Americans, determined by a yearly FREE physical, provide a tax benefit; either in the form of a return payment or adjustment in other insurance premiums. This will encourage our citizens to take a look inward to better physical fitness - if money motivates them in the least, which everyone knows it most definitely does.

11. Establish financial incentives for companies engaged in research and technologies that will help America become more self-sufficient, particularly in the natural energy arena.

12. Look in the mirror. If you like what you see, everyone else should too. If you don't, fix the one "house" you can!

YOUR OWN!

CANCER

What once was the most perplexing question in my life has turned into a source of disdain for the entire cancer complex that is growing, not coincidentally, like a cancer itself, particularly in the United States of America.

On August 17, 1989, my mother lost her struggle to stay alive. Cancer won. And I thought that was just the way it was supposed to end for her. Hindsight is always 20/20, but had I a scintilla of an inkling as to what the cancer industry was really like back then, I would have put up a bigger fight to make sure that she did not subject herself to the "conventional treatments" that were available.

Think about it. That was 1989. We are STILL trying to find a cure for cancer? Are you kidding me? I insist we are not trying to find a cure for cancer; we're trying to raise trillions of dollars to SAY we're trying to find a cure for cancer. That is why the American Cancer Society (ACS) is the largest "non-profit" organization in the world! All the uninformed among us are just hoping against hope; because we don't want to see anyone or any more of those we love and cherish, perish.

If cancer was really cured it would end an industry that has managed to have its say over our lives for over a century. If cancer was really cured, millions of people would lose their jobs. If cancer was really cured, the research community would have to find other diseases to fight – but there would be no bigger cash cow than cancer, not even close. Not ever!

The ACS relies on what I call "fear funds" from Americans who are desperate to find the answer to cancer. Folks like friends, acquaintances, mothers, fathers, sisters, brothers, cousins, uncles, aunts, nephews, nieces, girlfriends, boyfriends, grandmothers and grandfathers send in checks by the boatload so that the ACS can continue its work to "find the cure."

In short, *everyone* knows s*omeone* in *some way* affected by this despicable disease.

THIS **NOT** JUST IN, LADIES & GENTLEMEN:

THE AMERICAN CANCER SOCIETY SPENDS A BILLION DOLLARS A YEAR ON SALARIES, EXPENSES & GENERAL OPERATIONS - *AND MERE PENNIES OF EVERY DOLLAR ACTUALLY GO TOWARD FINDING A CURE FOR CANCER!*

LET ME REPEAT THAT:

THE AMERICAN CANCER SOCIETY SPENDS A BILLION DOLLARS A YEAR ON SALARIES, EXPENSES & GENERAL OPERATIONS - *AND MERE PENNIES OF EVERY DOLLAR ACTUALLY GO TOWARD FINDING A CURE FOR CANCER!*

Mr. John Seffrin became the president of the ACS on December 21, 2009 and as of this writing remains its president. With benefits and deferred compensation, his annual salary is $1,045,887.00. The funny thing about

152

cancer is…if the ACS found a cure for it, no matter where John might end up – you can bet he'll take a MAJOR pay cut.   Since so many people die of cancer (and I don't wish that disease on anyone) wouldn't it be ironic if Mr. Seffrin did too - while "trying to find its cure?" I'm just sayin!

Right!   Here I am again with another one of my conspiracy theories, you might suggest.   But let me extend this argument beyond the ACS.

There is a doctor alive today that runs a cancer treatment center in Houston, Texas that bears his name; *The Burzynski Clinic*.   His clinic was open for business when my Mom was going through the last phase of her life.

NOBODY knew about Dr. Stanislaw Burzynski or his clinic then, because the government wanted to make sure that his discovery of **antineoplastons** (natural anticancer agents found in the blood of healthy people but mysteriously absent in the blood of people with cancer) did not become widely, if at all, known.

That would make sense too, because a cure that is NATURALLY derived would be far more detrimental to the cancer "machine" that drives our medical society and employs so many thousands here in America.

Additionally, how could they then justify billions of dollars in grant money, building more ACS office complexes (which number over 900 as of 2011) or paying million dollar salaries to people like John Seffrin?

153

Unfortunately for the ACS, the Internet will not allow this secret to be kept any longer. You can learn all about the good doctor's scientific breakthroughs simply by going to the following website: www.BurzynskiClinic.com or by calling their toll-free number 800-714-7181 or outside the U.S. at: +1 713 335 5697 and having a conversation with one of their qualified Cancer Information Specialists.

This I know for certain: Had I or any of my family members known about the Burzynski Clinic back in 1988, even though it might have been a fledgling operation, we definitely would have opted to take Mom *there* instead of Tijuana, Mexico; where people desperately flocked in those days for laetrile treatments...because the F.D.A. wouldn't dare approve the naturally occurring-substance found mainly in the kernels of apricots, peaches and almonds. Too readily available to the public is not good business for the cancer industry!

In my own country, ***where we supposedly enjoy freedom and liberty that we keep fighting overseas to guarantee*** - a person cannot and dare not get involved with experimental treatment of any kind; even if it's in an effort to save ones own life... if said treatment is not sanctioned or approved by the F.D.A.

To me, that is an unmitigated crime.

The F.D.A. is a private corporation, not a governmental organization, yet they are not held to any governmentally imposed standards or regulations.

As always, it's about: BIG Pharma, BIG Oil, BIG Business and certainly BIG Cancer - which always spells BIG $.

If cancer manages to make its way inside of my body, they'll have to jail or shoot me before I will let anyone dictate the treatment I am to receive; whether it is considered conventional, experimental or perceived as utter quackery!

More and more information is coming out on a near daily basis which points to natural eating and other healthful life patterns as ways to *avoid getting cancer*.

Subscribe to Mike Adams' Natural News newsletter at www.NaturalNews.com and have your eyes opened wider than ever with regard to what you can do to naturally reduce your risks of getting cancer and to increase your longevity.

My biggest hero of all time is the late, great fitness guru, Francois Henri LaLanne; better known to anyone who's lived any number of years in the 20th century as "Jack LaLanne" who famously lamented:

"If man made it, don't eat it!"

Truer words have never been spoken. Jack made it to 96 years of age, drinking juice with their "natural" skin still enveloping them as they were squeezed through his magical juicer. He performed feats well into his eighties that would fall mere mortals in their early twenties.

To hear him talk so basically about cancer and all other diseases, understanding his feeling about naturally avoiding all of it - made you feel like a total idiot for blindly following the advice of medical practitioners on so many matters concerning personal health.

Rest in peace, Sir!

Jack LaLanne (September 26, 1914 – January 23, 2011)

And on the heels of the natural ways to health, I give you the following sarcastic and totally antithetical poem:

BUT FIRST, THESE BRIEF DISCLAIMERS

Each time you see commercials about drugs for sale...
clear visions of side effects somehow prevail.

Take for example most hay fever or ragweed drugs...
I don't think they've managed to iron out all their bugs.

May cause rectal leakage and even sudden death...
STOP taking if you experience shortness of breath.

May cause headaches, depression and redness for days...
STOP taking if you find you've entered this phase.

May cause nausea, vomiting and an uncontrollable tic...
STOP taking if you notice the skin falling off of your

May cause you to lose the last hair on your head...
STOP taking and try baby aspirin instead.

May cause your erection to last a whole year...
STOP taking if you happen to hold your wife dear.

May cause anxiety, tension and make you all stressed...
STOP taking if bleeding occurs when y'all get dressed.

May cause pneumonia, strep throat and even the gout...
STOP taking altogether...just toss the crap out!

If you must ignore these disclaimers and throw a few back...
be grateful you're not addicted to mescaline or crack!

Let's name a few brands for the sake of my readers...
especially for those who wish to be breeders.

Listed alphabetically from letter **A** all the way up to **Z** …
the side effects are listed at their websites for all to see.

Adderall is a psycho-stimulant that keeps you awake…
causing seizures only felt inside a 6.9 earthquake.

Amoxicillin may cause liver damage, yellow eyes and skin…
yeast infection and hives that just might do you in.

Unexplained swelling of the lips, mouth or throat…
acute pancreatitis, your worst nightmare compote.

Cymbalta may cause canker sores & suicidal notions…
rapid heart rate, hallucinations and internal commotions.

Cipro may cause you to react in a confusional state…
this synthetic concoction makes spasms elevate.

Prednisone may cause headaches, insomnia and bowel disease…
Headaches I can handle, but bowel disease? PLEASE!

Prozac, the treatment for anxiety disorder is scary…
itching, tightness in the chest, its side effects vary.

Zoloft causes dry mouth, dizziness and decreased sexual drive…
makes you wonder if taking it is worth staying alive.

STOP taking any of these if you notice blood in your stools…
or run the risk of dying young as one of life's biggest fools.

I share these disclaimers with you for one simple reason…
so you'll blow up your medicine cabinet this coming flu season!

CRAZY PEOPLE

In 1990 the film *Crazy People* was released, starring Dudley Moore, Paul Reiser and Daryl Hannah. It is high on my TOP TEN list of comedies.

Here's its tagline: *A bitter ad executive who has reached his breaking point, finds himself in a mental institution where his career actually begins to thrive with the help of the hospital's patients.*

The late, great actor and virtuoso jazz pianist, Moore, portrays ad exec, Emory Leeson, who has basically become completely burned out as a result of his inability to come up with catchy slogans that "SELL!"

He decides to do something totally off the wall and outside-the-box…tell the truth about the products he represents. And the new campaign turns out to be a huge success.

Some of the ads:

"Volvo — they're boxy but they're good."

"Jaguar — for men who'd like hand-jobs from beautiful women they hardly know."

And this one for a Greek travel agency:

"Forget Paris. The French can be annoying. Come to Greece. We're nicer."

An ad for a new horror flick called *The Freak* insists: "It won't just scare you; it will fuck you up for life!"

The mere concept of **truth in advertising** sends shutters up and down the spine of any marketing executive, and there can simply be **none of it** in our society.

Why?

Because we are a society that thinks if we use "dirty words" in public the people will be offended - and offended people won't buy products from dirty-minded or dirty-speaking companies.

What a load of bullshit!

How is it that for all intents and purposes we seem to be advancing exponentially in the fields of technology and research yet remain mired in puritanical ethos when it comes to language or the human body?

George Carlin's 1972 list of 7 words you weren't allowed to broadcast over the airwaves was a comedy skit, but, by nature, was and still is an indictment on our basic freedom of speech as guaranteed in some important document of the 1770's.

40 years later, only piss and tits are allowed. Shit, fuck, cunt, cocksucker and Motherfucker are still taboo.

They are JUST WORDS for crying out loud. If you've not lived under a rock your entire life you've no doubt read the hysterical and lengthy list of uses for the word fuck.

Once you use any word long enough you become desensitized and its meaning is diluted.

But dwell on a list of words *"you are forbidden to use"* and greater value, if not attention, is paid them; not due to the nature of the words themselves, but out of contempt for the temerity of those in charge of such things, chiefly the Federal Communications Commission (FCC), for imposing the ban in the first place.

Like the barring of alcohol in the early 1900's, prohibition of *anything* cannot work - because it is an attempt to take away our freedom; and we Americans don't take kindly to that sort of shit. Fuck no, we do not!

Rest in peace, George Carlin (May 12, 1937 - April 4, 2008)

The infamous "wardrobe malfunction" of Janet Jackson sent this country into such a tizzy because one of her "covered" nipples popped out of her costume (or Justin Timberlake yanked it out) that it was front-page headline material for weeks following Super Bowl XXXVII, played Sunday, February 1, 2004.

Instead of being remembered as the bright new facility that brought the biggest football game of the year to the world, Reliant Stadium in Houston, Texas became synonymous with the "wardrobe malfunction" and CBS nearly lost its broadcasting license over the flap, flip or flash!

All of this hoopla occurring over a single nipple being exposed? Actually we didn't even see the nipple under the pasty that was glued over it

Are you *freaking* serious FCC?

Come on, really people!

So, for purposes of a quick review:

We are recruited to fight and possibly die in wars we have no business fighting when we are 18 - yet cannot buy a beer when we come home on leave until 3 years later.

We are barred from uttering certain expletives or, heaven forbid, flashing a covered nipple or any other body part in public - but the powers that be have no problem with us viewing images of maiming and other atrocities of war.

I defy any authority figure to dare tell me that human nudity and "The F Bomb" are more offensive than guts spilling out before my eyes in Technicolor as the result of a real dropped bomb.

The image of Nguyên Văn Lém being shot in the head on LIVE TV during the Tet Offensive will never go away. It will haunt me forever.

Without knowing any of the back-story then, all I could see in my mind's eye was the moving picture of the fired shot - and the man crumbling to his instant death in the middle of the dirt road.

One can only imagine how the Australian photographer, Neil Davis, who was working as a cameraman for NBC News felt for the rest of his days after shooting that horrific video.

A porno flick I watched when I was 22 left no indelible images. Well, maybe a couple. It was a pretty good movie.

TIME FOR ANOTHER VERY BRIEF POLL:

1. Would you rather…

A. Watch pictures of people dying in war?
B. Use "The F Word" in an important teleconference?

I know you feel me on this one, folks. As always, the double standard imposed by the holier- than-thou crowd is in place and the "regular guys" out there like you and I - remain powerless to do anything other than write about it.

To say our freedoms are not eroding would be to deny that the world is round, that the planet is undergoing severe climate change or that the Detroit Lions will eventually win a Super Bowl.

Well, 3 out of 4 ain't bad.

They are a much improved team, though!

THIS JUST IN!

Mohammar Gadhafi or Kaddafi or Khadafy (or however your favorite media outlet spells it) was killed in a Libyan rebel raid on October 20, 2011. For a solid 24 hours the video of his body, proof of his demise, bombarded the airwaves. You could see the bullet entry point in his skull.

Now, if *those* images aren't more disgusting or as potentially emotionally scarring as witnessing a covered *nipple* for a millisecond, a *body part* that all humans have (although there's a real purpose for them on women) - I don't know *what* is!

Which of the following would you prefer seeing?

A. A deposed dictator's newly decomposing body?
B. Janet Jackson's fully exposed and rather lovely right breast for a millisecond?

Don't even answer that one.

Mohammar now joins fellow terrorists Osama bin Laden and Saddam Hussein; two other villainous chaps with over indulgent tendencies toward ultra-violence whose vivid ends were paraded in front of our eyes over international TV - in death.

I would be entirely remiss and politically incorrect if I did not pay homage by providing their eulogies too, so:

Rest in pieces, you despicably nefarious creatures!

Saddam Hussein (April 28, 1937 - December 30, 2006)

Osama bin Laden (March 10, 1957 - May 2, 2011)

Mohammar Gadhafi (June 7, 1942 - October 20, 2011)

And speaking of death...

PLEASE DON'T TALK
ABOUT ME WHEN I'M GONE

"He was such a wonderful man"
they say once you are gone.

Why do they wait until it's too late...
till you're buried in Forest Lawn?

"He left a lovely family and all his friends shall miss him;
to everyone on Earth he met, he was a man of vision!"

Perhaps if he had known all this before he up and died,
he might have stuck around a bit
to accept such fond replies.

We're always remembered for the beautiful things
but have to pass on first.

Why is brotherhood so difficult
to envision or to thirst?

Please don't talk about ME when I'm gone.

Besides, your friends will think you're nuts,
talking to a lawn!

THANK YOU

Words are personal.

Sometimes we're reluctant to share them.

Sometimes we wonder how they'll be perceived.

Sometimes they rub people the wrong way.

If any of my words offended you,
please know that was not even close to my intention.

If any of my words inspired you,
please know that was my every intention.

If any of my words motivated *you* to *write
that would be amazing!

*I can give no greater praise than to share with you a very special online company called Create Space. They make it simple to get your book printed and have the most helpful staff of support professionals imaginable. If you've ever dreamed of seeing your words in print, you owe it to yourself to check them out:

www.CreateSpace.com

I'd been contemplating putting my words in book form for a long time, and it feels great to see them snuggled together like this.

Thank you for reading this collection of poetry, random thoughts and general musings. I wish you all the best that life has to offer and hope that you are not, nor will you ever become, one of those people categorized in my poem, EXCUSES, EXCUSES!

35611603R00099

Made in the USA
Middletown, DE
09 October 2016